BROADCASTS
FROM THE BLITZ

Also by Philip Seib

Beyond the Front Lines:
How the News Media Cover a World Shaped by War

Campaigns and Conscience:
The Ethics of Political Journalism

The Global Journalist:
News and Conscience in a World of Conflict

Going Live:
Getting the News Right in a Real-time Online World

Headline Diplomacy:
How News Coverage Affects Foreign Policy

Taken for Granted:
The Future of U.S.–British Relations

BROADCASTS
FROM THE BLITZ

**HOW EDWARD R. MURROW
HELPED LEAD AMERICA INTO WAR**

PHILIP SEIB

Potomac Books, Inc.
Washington, D.C.

First Paperback Edition 2007.
Copyright © 2006 by Potomac Books, Inc.

Excerpts of the broadcasts, speeches, and writings of Edward R. Murrow are reprinted by permission of C. Casey Murrow. All rights reserved. Acknowledgment is gratefully made to the following for permission to reprint excerpts from these works: Little, Brown and Company and James Leutze for *The London Journal of General Raymond E. Lee*; PDF Literary Agency for *Britain Speaks,* by J. B. Priestley; Rivington Winant for *Letter from Grosvenor Square,* by John G. Winant; Mount Holyoke College Archives and Special Collections for the Edward R. and Janet Brewster Murrow Papers; the BBC for materials in the BBC Written Archives Centre; Chatham House for materials in the Royal Institute of International Affairs Archives; and Adam Nicolson for Harold Nicolson's *Diaries and Letters*.

Library of Congress Cataloging-in Publication Data

Seib, Philip M., 1949–
Broadcasts from the Blitz: how Edward R. Murrow helped lead America into war /
Philip Seib. – 1st ed.
p.cm.
Includes bibliographical references and index.
ISBN 978-1-59797-012-9 (hardcover: alk. paper)
1.   World War, 1939–1945—Journalism, Military. 2. World
        War, 1939–1945—Diplomatic history. 3. Murrow, Edward
        R. 4. Radio journalism—United States—History—20th
        century. 5. London (England)—History—Bombardment,
        1940–1941. I. Title.

D799.U6S45 2006
070.4'4994053—dc22

                                                                2005055223

ISBN 978-1-59797-102-7 (paperback: alk. paper)

Potomac Books, Inc.
22841 Quicksilver Drive
Dulles, Virginia 20166

First Edition

10   9   8   7   6   5   4   3   2   1

Dedicated to the memory of Marty Haag,
a wonderful friend and a journalist
in the Murrow tradition.

Contents

Preface   ix

Prologue   August 31, 1939   I

Chapter **1**   Radio Goes to War   7

Chapter **2**   Murrow's England   49

Chapter **3**   London Besieged   77

Chapter **4**   Yanks and Brits   115

Chapter **5**   "We Are All in the Same Boat Now"   147

Acknowledgments   175

Notes   177

Bibliography   197

Index   203

About the Author   209

Preface

From September 1939 until December 1941, Europe tore itself apart while the United States watched. Believing themselves to be safely distanced from the fighting, most Americans wanted no part of another war just two decades after the last one. This time, they thought, let the Europeans clean up their own mess.

One person who wasn't willing to be just a spectator was Edward R. Murrow. With the words "This is London," the CBS broadcaster arrived in Americans' living rooms straight from the war zone, bringing with him air raid sirens, bomb blasts, and stories of courageous Brits who would not be beaten into submission. After listening to Murrow in London, Americans started thinking: Maybe, just maybe, we should help them.

Murrow wanted Americans to rouse themselves, recognize the menace of Adolf Hitler, and come to the rescue of Britain, the last bulwark against Nazi conquest. He was just a journalist, but he realized he could use the young medium of radio to galvanize public opinion and push U.S. policymakers. He worked hard to make Americans aware of what was at stake and how the danger that seemed so distant now would soon threaten them. Murrow also assisted the British government's courtship of America, providing advice about how to best use radio's political power, and in one instance he helped secure American funding for a British intelligence operation that monitored other nations' radio broadcasts.

Should he have been doing all that? Given Murrow's standing as the patron saint of American journalism, questioning his ethics is uncommon, but the conventional rule is that journalists should report—not make—the news, and should keep their distance from those they cover. Objectivity should be paramount. After examining Murrow's on- and off-air work in London, those who rail against journalistic bias can argue that he abandoned neutrality and embraced partisanship.

But his defenders can point out, in hindsight, that he was on the side of the angels, sensibly warning America about Hitler's true intentions and recommending the wisest course of action—to promptly do whatever was necessary to stop Nazi Germany.

As a teacher of journalism and practicing journalist, I have long admired Murrow's skill as a broadcaster and his commitment to maintaining the highest standards of his profession. I think there was no ethical transgression by Murrow; a journalist who sees evil has a responsibility to alert the world to it. Journalists are the sentinels of conscience and in that role should not be totally constrained by objectivity, which is a useful but not absolute standard. Murrow moved in tandem with Franklin Roosevelt and Winston Churchill to push the United States away from its self-deluding notion that it could go its own way, safe amidst the world's storms. He did not see a need to divorce journalism from patriotism. In hindsight it is clear that Murrow's appraisal of Hitler and his opinion about American intervention were correct, and Americans were well served by his passionate commitment to both his journalism and his cause.

Others in the news business have stepped beyond reporting the news and affected public policy. During the 1890s, publishers William Randolph Hearst and Joseph Pulitzer so inflamed public opinion that President William McKinley slid into the Spanish-American War. Since Murrow's time, graphic television images of war, famine, and other horrors have influenced foreign policy through the "CNN effect." But Murrow's experience was special in a number of respects.

First, the stakes were incredibly high because of the magnitude of Hitler's threat as he built his empire and obliterated those who did not fit into his plans for the German Reich and its master race. Murrow frequently insisted that there was a moral duty to fight in order to stop the spread of this unprecedented evil.

Second, Murrow worked alongside giants. The political and rhetorical skills of Roosevelt and Churchill have rarely been matched by leaders before or since. Murrow knew both men well and formed an unspoken but firm alliance with them to reach their common goals of ensuring Britain's survival and bringing America into the war.

Murrow's broadcasts were haunting and inspiring, describing the import of the global struggle and the tenacity of individual Britons. Night after night, he told London's story after watching waves of attacking planes and picking his way through fiery, rubble-strewn streets. He was part of a journalistic community that included many of the profession's finest—Eric Sevareid, Charles Collingwood, Mollie Painter-Downes, Ernie Pyle, Larry LeSueur, Quentin Reynolds, and others.

Less visibly, he engaged in the politics behind the news. Privately and on the air, he made no secret of his dislike for advocates of appeasement, including American ambassador Joseph P. Kennedy, and although he frequently told his listeners in the United States that they must decide for themselves whether Britain was worth helping, his own views were obvious.

Understanding Murrow's journalism requires knowing something about this complicated man. When he came to London in 1937 to direct the European operations of CBS, he and his wife Janet were just in their twenties. Before and during the war, their love for London and their admiration for the British character never faltered, nor did their idealism as they watched democracy battle fascism. At work, Ed kept up a ferocious pace. He spent his days gathering news and wrapped up his broadcasts after midnight, then he prowled the streets to survey the latest damage inflicted by the Germans, and finally he returned home with perhaps a few journalists or politicians in tow to play poker, drink whisky, and talk through the day's events. He sometimes slipped into deep depression, particularly about his country's refusal to face reality, and he and Janet—like other Londoners—faced the constant pressures of life under siege.

While the dark poetry of Murrow's broadcasts helped focus Americans' attention on Britain's courageous stand, Roosevelt was adroitly moving the United States closer to war. He had to do so cautiously because isolationist sentiment, led by the likes of Charles Lindbergh, remained strong, and the president did not want to jeopardize his top priority—reelection in 1940. Murrow's reports about England's fight provided political cover for Roosevelt, because helping the noble Brits, as described by Murrow, was increasingly seen by American voters as being the right thing to do. Once the presidential election was past, Roosevelt increased aid to Britain and became more assertive in his dealings with Germany. In early 1941, the president said, "When you see a rattlesnake poised to strike, you do not wait until he has struck before you crush him."

When the Murrows returned to the United States for a visit in autumn 1941, Ed's courage and foresight were hailed by his colleagues and the public. Polls showed that Americans were waking up and recognizing that their interests required a closer alliance with Britain. During their stay, the Murrows were looking forward to seeing many of their friends, including Franklin and Eleanor Roosevelt, who had invited them to come by for a quiet Sunday supper on December 7.

Despite the events of that day, Eleanor insisted that they come. After dinner, while Ed sat with FDR in the president's study, Roosevelt opened up to Murrow about the extent of the losses at Pearl Harbor, which were far more devastating than the public had been told. Torn between his reporter's instincts and his loyalty to his friend, Murrow let the latter prevail. He told no one what the president had said to him that night until years later, after FDR had died and the war had ended.

The Roosevelt administration immediately tried to recruit Ed to help with its wartime broadcasting, but he and Janet were determined to return to London. With America in the war, there would be many more stories to tell from Britain, and besides, London was much closer to the action. Ed couldn't resist that.

Beginning with his broadcasts during the war's first days, Murrow's reporting contributed to the eventual defeat of Germany and so was a splendid achievement. He helped lead the United States into a war that could not be avoided and had to be won. Murrow in London did superb journalism and served his country well.

Prologue

August 31, 1939

War was coming to Great Britain. Neither courage nor cowardice could stop it now.

On August 25, 1939, England had entered into a treaty with Poland that formalized its pledge to stand by the Poles if they were attacked by Germany. Adolf Hitler paused and began meaningless negotiations with Poland, wanting not to secure peace but only to give Britain a chance to renege on its promise and get out of the way. Given the British government's recent record of retreating from confrontation, that seemed a likely outcome.

But the British had finally recognized that the previous year's Munich agreement had not brought about "peace for our time," as Neville Chamberlain had claimed, and that Hitler's promises were worthless. And so they abandoned appeasement and steeled themselves for the fight. Winston Churchill later wrote, "It is a curious fact about the British Islanders . . . that as danger comes nearer and grows they become progressively less nervous; when it is imminent they are fierce; when it is mortal they are fearless."[1]

While the British prepared, the United States watched or, more precisely, listened. At eleven in the morning New York time on this last day of peace, CBS correspondent Edward R. Murrow—a young man from Polecat Creek, North Carolina—gave Americans a sense of what it was like to be in England. "Can't you imagine for a moment," he asked, "that you are a member of a family living perhaps in Battersea? Here is what you would have heard in a broadcast just a short while ago, presented very calmly in a well-modulated English voice. It has been decided to start evacuation of school children and other priority classes." He described the plan: children should be sent to school the next day with extra clothing and gas masks. They would then go with their teachers to homes in safer areas outside London where families had offered to take them in. Parents were urged to let their children go and were assured that they would be told where the children were once they had reached their new homes. Murrow provided more details about how this would work—the names of the children were to be sewn into their clothing, emergency rations were being allocated, much of the railroad system would be used for the evacuation, and so forth.[2]

For the British, this was the war's first casualty: the family, now to be separated indefinitely. Think, Murrow asked his American listeners, what that must be like. His report resonated because it was not about politicians and their maneuvering, but about British fathers and mothers and children who were not so different from their counterparts in the United States.

Later that day Murrow was on the air again, reiterating that "tomorrow we shall see the children, the halt, the lame, and the blind going out of Britain's cities," with more than three million soon to be on the move. The government was still saying that war was not inevitable, but the Navy had been fully mobilized, and reservists were being summoned by the Army and the Royal Air Force. The previous night, said Murrow, the byword in London had been "Stand steady." Tonight, he said, it was "Prepare for action."[3]

❅   ❅   ❅   ❅

Murrow had arrived in London in April 1937 as CBS's European representative, responsible for finding topics and guests for the network's programs. During his first months on the job, his recruits for on-air appearances ranged from the BBC Singers to Ethiopian emperor Haile Selassie. Murrow was not broadcasting himself; he had no training or experience as a journalist and at this time the American radio networks relied on outsiders to comment on the news of the day. Murrow's job was to line up print journalists and others to analyze events.

As he settled into London life, Murrow quickly established himself in British journalistic and political circles. He presented a talk about "The International Aspects of Broadcasting" at the Royal Institute of International Affairs and began to work closely with the BBC.[4]

Radio was something of a novelty in terms of delivering breaking news from around the world, and its impact was still being evaluated, often critically. Around this time, *Variety* noted that "while it does not create the tensions of the day, radio elongates the shadows of fear and frustration. We are scared by the mechanized columns of Hitler. We are twice-scared by the emotionalism of radio. Radio quickens the tempo of the alternating waves of confidence and defeatism which sweep the country and undermine judgment. Radio exposes nearly everybody in the country to a rapid, bewildering succession of emotional experiences. Our minds and our moral natures just cannot respond to the bombardment of contradiction and confusion."[5]

That characterization of radio overlooked the medium's value as an information tool. Sound could give a message added intensity, but if those who delivered radio news were committed to their journalistic responsibilities, "emotionalism" would not distort their reports and listeners would not, presumably, respond with their own excessive emotion (as some had done during Orson Welles's broadcast of "The War of the Worlds" in October 1938). Also, radio was changing the public's attitude about the timeliness of news—the daily newspaper was just too slow when developments in a big story were shifting hour by hour. The appetite for the early version of "real-time news" was growing, and by 1939, more than 60 percent of Americans regularly listened to radio news programs.[6]

During its formative years, radio news was much like a newspaper article being read into a microphone. But sentences that

3

look fine on the printed page are not always comfortably spoken or heard. Murrow recognized that and helped change it. He delivered his first on-air report in 1938, broadcasting from Vienna as part of a hastily cobbled-together newscast about Germany's annexation of Austria. In the years to come, he brought vibrancy and spontaneity to his radio reporting that held listeners' attention and stirred their imagination. His colleague Howard K. Smith wrote that "Ed didn't know how to write like a newsman, which freed him to write with his own fresh eye and ear. I went through the files of his first broadcasts and they were just notes on paper. The man was ad-libbing transatlantic broadcasts!"[7]

Throughout the years before Pearl Harbor, Murrow's reports would urge Americans to carefully consider the European war and their country's role in it. He made more real a conflict that many in the United States still viewed as a remote struggle having little to do with them. How much influence he had cannot be measured precisely, but large numbers of people listened to him and they thought about what they heard. Presumably they used the information he provided as they made up their minds about the right course for their country. That is all a journalist can ask for.

The transforming power that Murrow brought to radio was largely a function of his complex personality, which was woven— almost always invisibly—into his broadcasts. His colleague Eric Sevareid cited Murrow's "strong, simple faiths and refined, sophisticated intellectual processes—poet and preacher, sensitive artist and hard-bitten, poker-playing diplomat, an engaging boy one moment and an unknowable recluse the next, a man who liked people in general and loved a few whom he held off at arm's length. . . . He could absorb and reflect the thought and emotions of day laborers, airline pilots, or cabinet ministers and report with exact truth what they were; yet he never gave an inch of himself away. His whole being was enmeshed in the circumstances of those days and events, yet he held his mind above them always."[8]

During those taut days of late summer 1939, Murrow and his CBS team in Britain and elsewhere in Europe were broadcasting four and five times a day, feeding shortwave reports to New York and from there across America. Their principal competitor, NBC, almost matched their output. The pace continued to increase: from August 22–29, CBS presented eighty-one broadcasts from Europe, NBC seventy-nine. On Sunday, August 27, alone, CBS had nineteen and NBC seventeen.[9]

But even while talk of war was smothering the last hopes for peace and London children were taking part in practice evacuations, Murrow's network bosses—like many other Americans—remained detached from the reality of the conflict that was about to begin. CBS told Murrow to organize a broadcast to be called "Europe Dances," which would be transmitted from cabarets in London, Paris, and Berlin. Murrow argued against such a frivolous venture at such a time, but the New York executives were unmoved. They and the American listeners, they believed, were more interested in dance music than in a European squabble. Finally, Murrow simply refused to do it.[10]

❊   ❊   ❊   ❊

Adolf Hitler, meanwhile, understood exactly how things stood. On August 31 he issued his "Directive Number One for the Conduct of the War," which said, in part: "Now that all the political possibilities of disposing by peaceful means of a situation on the Eastern frontier which is intolerable for Germany have been exhausted, I have determined on a solution by force. The attack on Poland is to be carried out in accordance with the preparation made. . . . The date of attack—September 1, 1939. Time of attack—04:45."[11]

Chapter 1

Radio Goes to War

As German forces tore through Poland, most Americans watched with detached distaste. The United States had come to the rescue in 1918 and there was little interest in doing so again. The Old World could resolve its own bloody quarrels.

But radio would not let America shut out the reality of what was happening. The airwaves brought to the United States the voices of Ed Murrow, Winston Churchill, and a few others who warned that the threat posed by Hitler and his Nazis extended beyond Europe.

When the war began, radio news was in its second decade, and as the sophistication of its technology and the quality of its journalism grew, so did its audience. In the United States in 1921, 60,000 homes had radios and there were thirty radio stations in the country. By 1940, there would be radios in more than twenty-nine million U.S. homes (out of a total thirty-five million households) tuned in to 814 stations.[1]

This meant that this new medium for journalism was reaching millions whose limited interest or literacy had previously kept them on the periphery of the news audience. Radio—as television and the Internet would later be—was a populist, democratizing force. Radio flowed into homes free of charge, and the national networks gave people something in common—information. Radio also brought an added vividness to news, taking its listeners into the midst of the action. Air raid sirens, antiaircraft fire, and bomb blasts were not merely described; they were heard in your own living room.

No formula existed for how this kind of news should be presented, so the war gave Ed Murrow and company the opportunity to shape their medium. They were able to do so partly because CBS increasingly relied upon its own staff members to broadcast the news, while principal rival NBC continued to use newspaper reporters, government officials, and others. *Variety* wrote that the CBS "family group" of correspondents was getting "closer to the human element, and they get to essentials quickly, interpret past and present as simply as possible for the ordinary listener." The newspaper hedged its initial appraisal of Murrow himself: "While less facile in speech than his colleagues, Murrow in London is always close to the dramatic and human element and furnishes an account which is clear and to the point."[2] *Variety's* critic was among those who didn't know what to make of Murrow. He clearly was not just another announcer; his voice did not have the polished neutrality that was radio's norm, but instead featured an intensity that warmed his soft-spoken delivery.

In 1939, Murrow was far from being the best known American broadcaster. Raymond Gram Swing, for one, had a huge worldwide audience, even though he had fewer U.S. listeners than did Murrow because he was carried by the Mutual network, which did not have the reach of CBS. Swing also reported from New York for the BBC, explaining America and American policy. It was estimated that 31 percent of the adult population in Britain listened to his broadcasts, and the BBC relayed his words to listeners throughout the British Commonwealth. He also contributed a "Weekly Cable on America" to the *London Sunday Express*, which had the largest circulation of any newspaper in the world.[3] In addition to Swing, William L. Shirer, H. V. Kaltenborn, and Elmer Davis were among the best known radio news voices of the time. But they remained detached; their listeners knew that their voices came to them from a studio. Murrow, too, used a studio, but he also took his microphone onto streets and rooftops, bringing dramatic vividness to his broadcasts. The live, on-scene television reporting of a later news generation had its roots in Murrow's work.

Fast and far-reaching, radio journalism was becoming more influential as news broadcasts became part of listeners' daily routines. Families listened together—it was not at all like passing the newspaper from person to person—and then they discussed what they had just heard. The newscaster was an electronic visitor, a combination of a media celebrity and a neighbor who dropped by to chat about the day's events. Murrow understood the importance of how news arrived in American homes. He knew that bombast wouldn't work; people grow impatient with loud speeches disguised as journalism. They want conversation and they want to know why the news matters—how it affects their lives. So Murrow followed the path of Franklin Roosevelt, who relied on a conversational style in his fireside chats. Rather than talking *at* people, he talked *with* them, as when he said in one of his radio addresses, "Let us sit down together, you and I, to consider our own pressing problems that confront us."

This was the approach Murrow wanted on CBS. Mary Marvin Breckinridge—a rare woman among "the Murrow boys"—remembered Murrow's instructions to her: Give the *human* side of the news; be neutral; be honest; talk like yourself. Murrow once noticed her suppressing a cough while she was on the air, and the next day he told her, "If you feel like coughing, go ahead and cough."[4] He wanted a naturalness that would pull listeners into the stories the journalists were telling.

Beyond broadcast style, Murrow was sensitive about maintaining balance in his reports. On September 1, 1939, as German forces swarmed into Poland and Britain did nothing beyond issuing one more ultimatum to Hitler, Murrow made clear that although he was appalled by the German aggression he was not accusing the British of dithering. He said that he was giving his listeners "such facts as are available in London tonight," and underscored his detachment: "I have an old-fashioned belief that Americans like to make up their own minds on the basis of all available information. The conclusions you draw are your own affair. I have no desire to influence them and shall leave such efforts to those who have more confidence in their own judgment than I have in mine."

Nevertheless, he added a note of commentary defending Britain's final attempts to avoid war: "I suggest that it is hardly time to become impatient over the delayed outbreak of a war which may spread over the world like a dark stain of death and destruction."[5] This was *his* view—not a newspaper editorial with no name attached to it—and he was delivering it directly to those who invited him into their living rooms. Given his willingness to insert such comments into his broadcasts, there was a certain disingenuousness in his "no desire to influence" claim.

Murrow often was close to the edge of CBS policy about avoiding advocacy. Murrow's boss, CBS director of public affairs Paul White, said, "The one thing that we have insisted upon above all else is as complete an objectivity as can be mastered." White cited a CBS memorandum that all the network's correspondents were told to read: "Columbia [Broadcasting System], as an organization, has no editorial opinions about what this country or any other country should or should not do. Those, therefore, who are its voice in presenting the news must not express their own feelings. In being fair and factual, those who present the news for Columbia must not only refrain from personal opinion, but must refrain from microphone manner designed to cast doubt, suspicion, sarcasm, ridicule or anything of that sort on the matter they are presenting. An unexcited demeanor at the microphone should be maintained at all times, though the tempo can of course be varied with the nature of the news. Dire forebodings, leaving the radio audience hanging up in the air and filled with suspense and terror of our creation, are not good broadcasting."[6]

In addition to these standards, CBS joined with NBC and Mutual to prepare guidelines for anyone doing on-air analysis: "No news analyst or news broadcaster is to be allowed to express personal editorial judgment or to select or omit news with the purpose of creating any given effect, and no news analyst or any other news broadcaster is to be allowed to say anything in an effort to influence action or opinion of others one way or the other." To prevent this from overly constraining their broadcasters, the networks added that "nothing in this is intended to forbid any news broadcaster from attempting to evaluate the news as it develops, provided he substantiates his evaluation with facts and attendant circumstances."[7]

Of course, the principle of strict noninvolvement was, and still is, unrealistic. In the news business, choices must be made about what to cover, how extensively to cover it, how prominently to present it, and so on. Reports about civilian casualties or refugees, for instance, will often have a predictable effect—a sympathetic response from at least part of the audience. The audience reaction may, in turn, have political effect as policymakers take note of shifts in public opinion. Murrow and some of his colleagues were sophisticated enough to recognize that they could exert this kind of influence, which could be amplified or modified by making subtle adjustments in the tone and substance of their reporting.

The networks' memo also reflected radio news executives' recognition that their medium possessed power different from that of newspapers. Paul White noted that "in a democracy there is virtually no limit to the number of newspapers that can be published. There is, however, a definite limitation to the number of possible radio stations because of the small number of frequencies available. Hence to permit any one individual a regular platform from which he could guide or attempt to guide the nation's thinking might constitute a fearful peril."[8]

Implementation of these policies varied. Sometimes the rules were applied vigorously, sometimes they were ignored. CBS would not air British singer Gracie Fields's rendition of five Shakespeare sonnets on Shakespeare's birthday because, said CBS, they contained "prophetic passages" about the war.[9] On the other hand, in one of his broadcasts in 1938, CBS news analyst H. V. Kaltenborn condemned "the Nazi Jew-baiters" who had "become a stench in the nostrils of peaceful decent men."[10]

The networks' caution was based on experience; radio had

been shown to be a powerful instrument in the hands of those who would "attempt to guide the nation's thinking." In the United States, Father Charles Coughlin, a Catholic priest who broadcast from the Shrine of the Little Flower in a Detroit suburb, first went on the air in 1926. He was an early supporter of Franklin Roosevelt ("The New Deal is Christ's Deal") but later accused Roosevelt of being in league with "godless capitalists, the Jews, communists, international bankers, and plutocrats." His political preaching on the radio attracted a huge audience; he received an average of 80,000 pieces of mail each week, and his criticism of the World Court in one broadcast generated 200,000 telegrams to the U.S. Senate. As he became increasingly controversial, CBS dropped him and he set up his own network. Eventually, much of his audience tired of his shrill anti-Semitism and by 1940 his clout had shriveled.[11]

Similarly, Louisiana politician Huey Long used radio to promote his "Share Our Wealth" plan and his slogan, "Every man a king, but no one wears a crown." James A. Farley, one of Roosevelt's top political advisors, said that Long's radio style was "a curious hodgepodge of buffoonery and demagogic strutting, cleverly bundled in with a lot of shrewd common sense and an evangelical fervor." Long claimed that he had support from 27,000 Share Our Wealth clubs with more than seven million members total. He gave six nationally broadcast speeches during the first three months of 1935 and received an average of more than 100,000 letters after each one. He was seen as a potent threat to Roosevelt's 1936 reelection chances before being assassinated in the Louisiana capitol building in September 1935.[12]

On a larger stage, Roosevelt, Hitler, and Churchill used radio with great effect to build political support and rally their countries. The medium was new enough that politicians, like media professionals, were still experimenting, not certain about how radio messages might affect the public. But what they knew—either through the young craft of audience research or just intuitively—led them to appreciate radio as a mobilizing tool.

Radio journalists were also coming to recognize this, and that was why Paul White and other news executives were careful about how they used an instrument that might profoundly alter public opinion. American news organizations' circumspect approach to coverage of the war in Europe, as articulated in their internal guidelines, mirrored Roosevelt's caution and the ambivalent attitude of the American public. News organizations also imposed limits on their war coverage because of costs incurred in staffing bureaus and displacing commercial programming. For a while, NBC and Mutual halted their coverage from all of Europe except Britain, and CBS reduced the number of its war bulletins and commentaries that did not have their own sponsors.[13]

But the CBS coverage picked up steam during the first months of the war. On a given night the network's "European Round Up" program, airing at 7 PM Eastern time, might feature conversations between a newscaster in New York (not yet referred to as an "anchorman") and correspondents in London, Berlin, Rome, Bucharest, and Washington. Everything was done live, and the overseas reporters had to rely on short-wave stations controlled by the governments of the countries they were in. The signal was picked up by RCA in New York and fed by land line to the CBS engineering headquarters, also in New York. From there it went by land line to the network's stations around the country, which used their individual transmitters to deliver the product to their listeners. As complicated as this sounds, the programming from Europe consistently conformed to a second-by-second schedule.[14]

In addition to the major networks' broadcasts from Europe, individual stations' war coverage also steadily grew. In April 1938, New York City stations carried ninety-seven scheduled news programs each week. By January 1940 the number was 187, and by June 1940 it was 253. Content for these reports was supplied primarily by the Associated Press, International News Service, United Press, and Transradio Press.[15] These numbers illustrate the growing amount of information at the disposal of the American public as opinions about the war were developing. Meanwhile, print coverage of the conflict was also expanding.

The effects of this flow of news on public awareness of events had to be recognized by those leading both sides of the debate about whether the United States should intervene and, if so, at what level. Exactly what impact the news reports would have on public opinion was unclear, particularly during the early months of the war, but the increasingly pervasive presence of information about events in Europe could not be discounted by those who made policy and those who wanted to influence it.

On September 3, 1939—two days after the invasion of Poland—British Prime Minister Chamberlain announced that "this country is now at war with Germany." Murrow reported that "the crowd outside Downing Street received the first news of war with a rousing cheer, and they heard that news through a radio in a car parked near Downing Street."[16] That night, King George VI spoke to the nation: "For the second time in the lives of most of us, we are at war. Over and over again we have tried to find a peaceful way out of the differences between ourselves and those who are now our enemies. But it has been in vain." The king's entry in his diary for that day reveals the trepidation that all but the most foolish felt when looking at what awaited the world. He recalled that when the First World War had begun in August 1914, he had been an eighteen-year-old midshipman, keeping watch on the bridge of a naval vessel in the North Sea. "We had been trained," he wrote, "in the belief that war between Germany and this country had to come one day, and when it did come we thought we were prepared for it. We were not prepared for what we found modern war really was, and those of us who had been through the Great War never wanted another. Today we are at war again, and I am no longer a midshipman in the Royal Navy."[17]

Across the Atlantic, Franklin Roosevelt used radio to explain that although the United States was not at war, Americans would face new challenges. "You must master at the outset," he said, "a simple but unalterable fact in modern foreign relations between nations. When peace has been broken anywhere, the peace of all countries everywhere is in danger." He promised to keep the United States out of the conflict—"Let no man or woman thoughtlessly or falsely talk of America sending its armies to European fields"—and reaffirmed America's neutrality, but with a caveat: "This nation will remain a neutral nation, but I cannot ask that every American remain neutral in thought as well. Even a neutral has a right to take account of facts. Even a neutral cannot be asked to close his mind or his conscience."[18] *Time* magazine noted that when the First World War began, Woodrow Wilson had said, "We must be impartial in thought as well as in action." *Time* liked Roosevelt's approach better: "Noble was the Wilsonian formula, and also nonsense, for no thinking man can fail to have convictions about the merits of the causes which plunge the world into war."[19]

Roosevelt carefully cloaked his first steps to aid Britain and France in his support for a revised Neutrality Act. The measure lifted an arms embargo and allowed belligerents to purchase American goods. They could do so only on a cash-and-carry basis and were required to use their own ships and crews to take them home. His stance was applauded by *Time* on the grounds that "1) This is 1939, not 1918; the U.S. embargo on arms to all belligerents gives Adolf Hitler almost the equivalent of an Atlantic fleet, because Great Britain and France can get no arms from the U.S. 2) Britain and France are fighting the fight of democracy against world revolution, are not just engaged in another imperialistic quarrel."[20]

Further editorial endorsements came from newspapers such as *The Kansas City Star:* "No legislation can automatically keep the United States out of war. But *The Star* agrees heartily with the President that the suggested changes in the neutrality laws would contribute toward peace at home and a better world order in Europe."[21] Support for FDR was far from universal; it was countered by isolationist voices, such as that of Socialist leader Norman Thomas, who said, "I do not doubt that the President formulated his policies with the best intentions in the world, but if I wanted to lead America straight into war, I would pursue the policies that he is following."[22]

At this stage, many in Europe and America assumed that

Germany would be promptly stopped by the combined might of England and France. Just before Britain went to war, King George reviewed the Reserve Fleet, which was manned by 12,000 naval reservists who had recently been called up. The review had provided Britons with a sense of pride and security: it was the greatest assembly of warships since 1914—133 ships in fifteen lines extending up to two nautical miles each.[23]

Despite belief that they could prevail, the British were bracing themselves. Office clerks loaded files to be shipped out of London to safe storage. Churches remained open day and night, with people dropping in for a few moments of prayer. As part of mobilization, it was announced that all men between the ages of eighteen and forty-one were eligible to be called for service. In anticipation of poison gas attacks, notices were posted about avoiding mustard gas contamination. For those now facing a confusing array of wartime sounds, a bit of doggerel was provided:

> "Wavering sound, go to ground.
> Steady blast, raiders past.
> If rattles you hear, gas you must fear.
> But if hand bells you hear, then all is clear."[24]

Murrow watched and reported, and although he is considered a staunch champion of the British cause, he was ambivalent about some characteristics of English life and was skeptical in the early days of the war about Britons' ability to work together. In one broadcast he said: "This is a class-conscious country. . . . The man with a fine car, good clothes, and perhaps an unearned income doesn't generally fraternize with the tradesmen, day laborers, and truck drivers. His fences are always up. He doesn't meet them as equals."

When Britain went to war, its economy was unsettled. At the beginning of 1939, two million Britons were out of work (out of a population of forty-seven million) and the National Unemployed Workers Union was visibly active. In 1938, to protest disparities in wealth, the union had sent one hundred members to order tea at London's Ritz Hotel, and just before Christmas two hundred members lay down on Oxford Street in the midst of affluent holiday shoppers.[25]

The class distinctions that Murrow noted were certainly not unique to Britain, and he reported that when the air raid siren sounded and people headed for the shelters, those distinctions tended to become irrelevant. But the lack of egalitarianism bothered Murrow; it was a theme he returned to. For example, after the war had been underway for almost a year, he observed that "this country is still ruled by a class," and he wondered if members of the ruling class really understood and trusted their fellow citizens.[26] The British were sensitive to such criticism and in their own broadcasts set out to affirm their commitment to democracy. In one radio commentary, novelist Sir Hugh Walpole said that England would "never be a snobbish country again. Class differences are breaking down everywhere, and for good."[27] That was a politically attractive, if unrealistic, message.

In addition to reporting breaking news, Murrow gave his listeners a sense of England's wartime mood. He took note of the changes brought about by the evacuations from London: "It's dull in London now that the children are gone. For six days I've not heard a child's voice. And that's a strange feeling." He talked of the loneliness in the homes from which children had departed and parents' mixed feelings—missing their children but glad that they were safely away.

He also gave his listeners a sense of London as place—changes in the look and pace of the city's life. Taxicabs, he said, didn't cruise the city any more; to conserve fuel they waited for passengers to come to them. In a park, green canvas chairs sat wet and unused near piles of sand ready to be put into sandbags. On Harley Street, "House to Let" signs were tacked to doors. Expensive shops on Bond Street were sandbagged, "the windows boarded up, others crisscrossed with strips of brown paper to prevent shattering." Tailor shop windows were full of uniforms; "they used to display well-cut dinner clothes and tweed sport jackets." The clothing stores offered "siren suits"—one-piece zippered attire that could be slipped on quickly when the air raid sirens sounded. At Trafalgar Square, he noted, "Admiral Nelson continues to look down from the top of his tall column. He seems almost out of place without a tin helmet and a gas mask."[28]

Murrow's own environment had also changed. The BBC's Broadcast House, from which CBS broadcast, was quickly transformed. By the morning of September 3, gas-tight doors and sandbags were in place. Most of the BBC's divisions were dispersed, leaving only its news operations in the heart of London.[29]

As Britain's war effort gained traction, Chamberlain inspired little confidence, and attention was focusing more and more on the First Sea Lord, Winston Churchill. Murrow reported in early October 1939 about a speech in which Churchill said that "all the courage and skill which the Germans always show in war will not free them from the reproach of Nazism, its intolerance and brutality." Murrow said that his British friends thought it was the best speech by a cabinet member since the war had started and that it "has increased Mr. Churchill's reputation as a leader. He, more than anyone else in this government, has been right in his predictions of European governments during the last several years." Murrow added that Churchill had not mentioned "any possibility of a patched up peace." The *Daily Telegraph* said of Churchill, "This was the voice of Britain speaking."[30]

Murrow wasn't the only American journalist to treat Churchill as a dominant figure. In the fall of 1939, Time, Inc. chairman Henry R. Luce ordered that a *Time* cover featuring comedian Jack Benny be scrapped—even though a million had been printed—and replaced with one picturing Churchill.[31]

Murrow knew that during Britain's shift from appeasement to war, forceful leadership—certainly more resolute than Chamberlain's efforts had been—would be essential, and he liked what he saw in Churchill. Years later, Murrow wrote about the power of Churchill's rhetoric: "He can produce a thunderous phrase with an impromptu air, although the phrase has obviously been well rehearsed and calculated. But his was the honor of marshaling and mobilizing the English language in such fashion as to sustain those upon whom the long dark night of tyranny had descended, and to inspire those who had yet time to arm themselves and beat it off."[32]

❋   ❋   ❋   ❋

Predicting the twists and turns of American policy was a high-stakes task for European officials, and they searched the news media for hints about where that policy might be heading. Murrow's words were scrutinized by a select audience beyond his American listeners. He reported that "machinery has been set up to study the trend and tone of American broadcasting and newspapers."[33] So when Murrow praised an anti-Nazi speech by Churchill, there were those in London, Berlin, and elsewhere paying attention. When influential U.S. newspapers such as *The New York Times* commented about the war, they too were certain to be read by Europe's policymakers. On September 2, a *Times* editorial said that Germany "has used its strategic position in the center of Europe to blackmail and to terrorize the small countries on its borders. . . . In the very act of its present resort to force against Poland it has given the lie to the most recent assurance of its respect for the decent standards of international conduct."[34]

British monitoring of American news coverage was one facet of a sophisticated campaign to pull the United States into the war, if not as a combatant at least as a provider of substantial aid. Because of uncertainty about what direction American policy might be taking, considerable tension existed in the transatlantic relationship. British officials were concerned that the United States would use its leverage to dictate post-war changes in British policy, particularly related to its far-flung empire. Chamberlain, in a letter to his sister, said, "Heaven knows I don't want the Americans to fight for us—we should have to pay too dearly for that if they had a right to be in on the peace terms."[35] Murrow reported that he heard comments such as, "Protect us from a German victory and an American peace," and "The Americans wish us well, want us to win the war, but without interfering in any way with their business or profit." Critics claimed that even when U.S. aid was provided, American factories—well out of harm's way—would use the influx of funds from the desperate British and French to expand their operations and profits.[36]

Anglo-American tensions also affected news coverage of the war, and Murrow and other American journalists repeatedly collided with British bureaucrats. U.S. broadcasters asked that a microphone position be set up somewhere in the Palace of Westminster so information from the House of Commons could quickly be relayed to the American audience. After thinking about the request for a week, the House Speaker said no—other foreign journalists would then have to be similarly accommodated and there just wasn't room for a microphone. The Admiralty also refused to allow access, saying "the granting of any facilities to the Americans was just a waste of time."[37]

Murrow was frustrated and although he didn't take the lack of cooperation personally, he disliked inefficiency and believed that such bureaucratic lethargy would take its toll on Britain's mobilization. One official of the British Ministry of Information observed that "Ed Murrow is getting more cynical in his attitude towards our war effort."[38]

Some British officials recognized the importance of maintaining an ample flow of information to America. Roger Eckersley, who directed the BBC's American Liaison section, lobbied for better access for U.S. radio correspondents (noting that they liked to be called "warcasters") and argued that their broadcasts "are listened to by a mass of sentimental, friendly people eager for news, and, subconsciously at all events, glad of Allied success and anxious for them to win the war. . . . Broadcasting can play an enormously important part" and was "a sure way of enlisting American sympathy and support." Eckersley asked for help from Churchill (at this time still at the Admiralty) concerning reporters' access to officials and front-line locations, telling him that "I feel sure that you will agree that it is a good thing to project as far as we can, without giving any indication of propaganda as such, the activities of this country and a picture of its war effort into the minds of American listeners, and to this end I am anxious to get as many facilities for them as I possibly can." Churchill responded that he would be happy to make coverage opportunities available, but he insisted that established bureaucratic process had to be respected: requests to him at the Admiralty needed to come through the Ministry of Information rather than directly from the Americans.[39]

Eckersley also lobbied Frank Darvall at the Ministry of Information, asking that American correspondents be given permanent passes to gain entry to restricted areas such as places that had been bombed.[40] When Murrow was unable to secure permission to visit British coastal defenses, Darvall tried to help: "Could the War Office be reminded of the immense importance of meeting this type of request quickly and fully? We and they ought to be begging the American radio chains to carry material about our preparedness, not resisting their efforts to do so."[41]

The BBC's Written Archives include many letters and memos about assisting American correspondents. One, for example, cites the objective of getting "the maximum amount of time devoted to broadcasts from Britain on the American networks with a view to familiarizing American listeners with the situation in this country and thus enlisting their sympathy on our side." Another memo notes that resolving access problems was tied to general principles, "the chief of which is to what extent broadcasting is viewed by the Government as a definite force in war, to be used, on the advice of experts, to the best possible advantage. Obstruction is still met with in certain directions—not individual obstruction but based on policy grounds."[42] This theme, which appears in this and similar documents from the BBC and others working with broadcasters, underscores the uncertainty about radio's influence. Some officials sensed they had a valuable political tool at hand, but they weren't sure how powerful it really was or how to use it.

As an adjunct to the work of its government agencies, Britain was building a substantial effort to influence world opinion. The International Propaganda and Broadcasting Enquiry, also known as the Channels of Publicity Enquiry, was funded by the British Secret Service and led by Ivison MacAdam, a close friend of Murrow and the secretary of the Royal Institute of International Affairs, a private organization similar in mission and status to the Council on Foreign Relations in the United States. The American section of this effort was chaired by Sir Frederick Whyte, who believed that the best way to affect U.S. public opinion was to entrust the delivery of Britain's message to American news organizations, which would minimize American fears about being manipulated by propaganda. Whyte was in regular contact with Murrow and appeared frequently on CBS broadcasts, explaining British affairs to the American audience.[43]

While MacAdam and Whyte tried to improve American journalists' working conditions, Murrow reciprocated by helping the BBC. Even before the war began, he contributed to news and other programs, such as the "Senior Geography" series of the Schools Broadcast Department, for which he did two broadcasts about immigrants' lives in America. He continued to accept BBC invitations whenever his schedule allowed and he turned down payments for his appearances, usually asking that the money be sent instead to war-related British charities.[44]

For Britain and the rest of Western Europe, the first months of war were known as "the phony war" or, as Chamberlain called it, "twilight war" because Britain and France did not attack Germany and Germany occupied itself primarily with chewing up Poland. An early instance of "real war" occurred at sea when a German submarine torpedoed the British passenger liner *Athenia* on the first day of the war, killing 112 persons, including twenty-eight Americans. The Germans denied responsibility and accused Churchill of personally ordering a bomb to be placed aboard the ship to provoke American retaliation against Germany.

Churchill, still excluded from the government's inner circle but eager for action, called this period "a prolonged and oppressive pause," and disdainfully said, "We contented ourselves with dropping pamphlets to rouse the Germans to a higher morality."[45] There was no good reason to believe that Hitler's appetite had been sated, but many in Britain began to relax. In London, evacuated children started to return; by mid-November more than 100,000 had come home.[46] Murrow was certain that a terrible storm would occur after this lull. He told his listeners that food rationing was about to be introduced in Britain; he also noted that the Norwegian Nobel Committee "has decided not to award a peace prize for 1939."[47]

The audience for Murrow's reports, as well as the target of British opinion-shaping efforts, was an American public caught up in fierce political debate about what the nation's role in the world should be, which was to be a dominant issue in the 1940 presidential campaign. Despite cultural and historical ties to Britain, there was still much support among Americans for Thomas Paine's observation nearly two centuries earlier that for America to be tied to England would be "like Hector to the chariot wheel of Achilles, to be dragged through all the miseries of endless European wars."

In the United States, two opposing interest groups—the Committee to Defend America by Aiding the Allies, and the America First Committee—helped shape the debate about intervention. By November 1940, the Committee to Defend, which was chaired by journalist William Allen White, had 750 chapters with 10,000 members. America First concentrated not on grass roots organization but on publicizing its view that America should prepare to defend itself rather than aid others.[48] Senator Gerald Nye, a North Dakota Republican and prominent isolationist, wrote: "We are selfish in our interest in America and for that which may be good for America. . . . Let Europe resolve its own difficulties. Let us recognize that we cannot hope to resolve them and that our attempts to do so result only in cost to ourselves without gain for Europe."[49]

Charles Lindbergh—the quintessential American hero in the eyes of many—was the isolationists' most visible and provocative champion. From late 1940 through most of 1941, the debate about intervention continued with increasing intensity. "As each side fought for the soul of the nation," wrote Lindbergh biographer

A. Scott Berg, "the argument boiled down to eleven months of oratory between Franklin Roosevelt and Charles Lindbergh." Lindbergh, who was a star attraction at rallies attended by thousands, argued against aiding England because it would prolong the war, which he thought should be settled through prompt negotiations with the Germans. He argued that U.S. entry into the war "would be the greatest disaster this country has ever passed through."[50] In a radio speech soon after the war began, Lindbergh said, "This is not a question of banding together to defend the white race against some foreign invasion. This is simply one more of those age-old struggles within our family of nations—a quarrel arising from the last war."[51]

Lindbergh's statements became more controversial as months passed. He claimed that "the only reason that we are in danger of becoming involved in this war is because there are powerful elements in America who desire us to take part," and in a later speech he identified the Roosevelt administration, the British, and Jews as the three groups "pressing this country toward war."[52]

Roosevelt limited his comments about America First, but his supporters pounced on every misstep by Lindbergh and others. Journalist Walter Winchell said that "Lone Eagle" Lindbergh should instead be known as "Lone Ostrich." Charges and countercharges about anti-Semitic, pro-Nazi sentiments were common, and, as happens with many important issues, the precise points of substantive debate were often lost in the glare of political fireworks. Radio was an important tool for groups involved in the intervention battle. The networks had guidelines that prevented politically controversial content from being aired, but America First escaped these restrictions by labeling their events for broadcast as "nonpartisan," which the National Association of Broadcasters agreed was the case. By fall 1940, NBC had carried fifteen America First rallies.[53]

Murrow's broadcasts offset some of the impact of speeches by Lindbergh and other isolationist leaders. Rallies and special broadcasts undoubtedly had effect, but Murrow was in the American living room almost every day. Journalism changes opinion in small increments, and Murrow's depictions of Europe's peril and Hitler's menace were effective partly because they were heard so frequently.

Although speeches at mass meetings and other forms of proselytizing captured plenty of attention, Americans remained detached as they watched events unfold during the war's first year. An advertisement for *The American Home* magazine captured the naïve nonchalance that was so common. The ad's headline was, "Hitler Threatens Europe—but Betty Havens' Husband's Boss Is Coming to Dinner, and *That's* What *Really* Counts." The copy, in part, read: "Yesterday, at bridge club, she did herself proud on the European situation. And it wasn't all out of the newsreels, radio bulletins and picture magazines she sees and hears, either. She quoted *Mein Kampf* with a guttural accent . . . admitted she'd hate to raise a totalitarian family! But today she's facing a crisis at home: Fred's boss is coming to dinner with his duchess! Perhaps they'll be mildly surprised at her knowledge of fact and fiction. *What really* counts, however, is their impression of her living room scheme in blue and plum. . . ."[54]

While Betty entertained the boss, U.S. news organizations were reporting the preliminary stages of the Holocaust, with newspapers describing the deportations of Jews from Vienna and elsewhere and their relocation into concentration camps. As early as 1939, *The New Republic* was describing "human suffering . . . beyond the compass of the imagination."[55]

And still many Americans had not decided whether a European conflict was any of America's business. This extended to policies about refugees. In March 1940, *Time* magazine noted that so far Americans "had shown no inclination to do anything for the world's refugees except read about them." Congress was considering seventy proposed bills that would keep immigrants out of the country, send them back where they had come from, or at least make it difficult for them to stay.[56] Journalist Vincent Sheean, who had been in London with Murrow and returned to the United States for a lecture tour, later wrote that "the depth of American unconcern in the first winter of the war was immeasurable. . . .

The general attitude toward the gathering storm was one of al-most inconceivable apathy."[57] But the British ambassador to the United States, Lord Lothian, thought that pro-British sentiment was slowly growing. He wrote to a friend in England, "There is a rising feeling that the U.S. is playing an unworthy part in one of the great dramas of history, and is in danger of losing her soul unless she shoulders her share of the burden."[58]

Some journalists did take sides in the debate—or at least were perceived as doing so. Raymond Gram Swing was active in in-terventionist groups.[59] Murrow was thought by at least some of his listeners to be advocating intervention, and he delightedly showed friends a letter from an isolationist addressed to "Ed-ward R. Moron."[60] Elmer Davis's evolving position reflected the unsettled nature of American opinion as the chances of a Ger-man victory seemed to grow. In an article for *Harper's* in early 1940, Davis wrote that "the interest of the American people re-quires us to keep out of the war for two sound reasons: We have unfinished business of our own to solve; and furthermore, past experience makes it doubtful that we could do Europe much good." But just a few weeks later, he said on a CBS broadcast: "The unrecognized premise of a good deal of American isola-tionism was a conviction that the Allies were going to win any-way so we needn't worry about how the war would come out. That conviction, recently, has been shaken; and accordingly a lot of people are worrying for the first time."[61]

But Davis, Lord Lothian, and others who professed to see America moving toward intervention may have overestimated the extent of that worrying about the war's outcome. By mid-1940 there did not appear to be any pronounced shift in senti-ment toward supporting intervention and there seemed to be little acknowledgment that America might find itself pulled into the war despite its efforts to stay out.

Vincent Sheean wrote that during his 1940 lecture tour in the United States, "I talked of the war, only of the war, its origins, nature, and course up to now; but it proved impossible to im-press upon any audience the supreme and almost exclusive importance of the subject. In the first place, nobody in my audiences anywhere seemed to realize how great the danger was; it was inconceivably remote to most of them, barely apparent to others. There was a certain amount of sentimental pro-English feeling . . . and there was a general dislike of the Nazis; but of realization that we were the ultimate enemy of both Germany and Japan, that we must fight, that we had no choice in the matter—of this there was not a trace." He added this anecdote: "One night in Albany a lady rose from her seat at question time and said to me: 'From what you have said I gather that you think Germany can win this war. Have I understood you correctly?' I replied, 'You certainly have.' The lady laughed aloud as she sat down, and a refined titter spread from her to other parts of the assembly."[62]

Hopes that Germany might back down or that Hitler might be removed by a coup stayed alive during the phony war, but when Germany unleashed its blitzkrieg, the reality of Hitler's intentions and German military superiority became shockingly clear. On April 9, 1940, Germany invaded Denmark and Norway. Denmark quickly surrendered while Norway fought on, but Allied attempts to support the Norwegians failed. On May 10, German troops rolled into Belgium, the Netherlands, and Luxembourg. At the end of May, the British Expeditionary Force was driven to the coast by the Germans and began its escape from Dunkirk. By June 14, the Germans were in Paris.

All that within ten weeks. And yet the most important development during that time may have occurred not on the battlefield but in London, where Neville Chamberlain's support finally dissolved and he was replaced on May 10 by Winston Churchill. The new prime minister quickly showed what lay ahead in terms of policy and rhetoric when he vowed to wage total war and declared, "I have nothing to offer but blood, toil, tears, and sweat." Murrow's evaluation of the new leader reflected what was to be lasting admiration: "He enters office with the tremendous advantage of being the man who was right. He also has the advantage of being the best broadcaster in this country. Mr. Churchill can inspire confidence. And he can preach a doctrine of hate that is acceptable to the majority of this country. That may be useful during these next few months."[63]

Two weeks later, Churchill faced the decision of whether to try to make a deal with Germany, as was recommended by his foreign secretary, Lord Halifax, and others. Churchill, who had consistently seen Hitler as an enemy who had to be fought, not negotiated with, rallied support within his cabinet against the Halifax position. He also kept an eye on the United States, telling the War Cabinet that taking a bold stand against Germany would command the Americans' admiration and respect. Churchill won this political battle; there would be no deal with Hitler.[64]

Churchill was taking his bold stand while much of his army was stranded across the Channel. In the face of the German onslaught, the Belgian army had surrendered, as had a large part of the French army. The British had been pushed onto the beaches at Dunkirk and faced almost certain capture or annihilation. The situation was so dire that Churchill felt it necessary to send a confidential memorandum to top government officials: "In these dark days the Prime Minister would be grateful if all his colleagues in the Government . . . would maintain a high morale in their circles; not minimizing the gravity of events, but showing confidence in our ability and inflexible resolve to continue the war till we have broken the will of the enemy to bring all of Europe under his domination."[65]

The evacuation from Dunkirk remains one of the most remarkable achievements in military history. More than 800 English boats—some of them naval vessels but most of them fishing and pleasure craft—shuttled back and forth across the Channel and rescued astonishing numbers of troops day after day. On May 29, 47,000 men were brought home; on May 30, 53,800; on May 31, 68,000; on June 1, 64,400; and over the next few days tens of thousands more. By June 5, the total was more than 338,000, including 125,000 French soldiers.[66]

Murrow reported that the British armed forces had "gilded defeat with glory," but, he added, the success of the retreat was no reason to think that Britain was now well prepared to carry on. "There is no disposition here," he said, "to conceal the fact that the British Expeditionary Force was inadequately equipped with armor and with guns, and above everything else they didn't have sufficient aircraft. The responsibility for this state of affairs rests squarely upon the men who led this country until a few weeks ago. They purchased a few months of normal living and normal working, while assuring the country that all was well and that time was on the side of the Allies. But they bought that quiet and complacency in an expensive market."[67]

The British were fond at this time of quoting William Pitt's observation that "England will save herself by her exertions and Europe by her example." But behind the bravado there was abundant pessimism. Although Churchill had quieted the most prominent defeatists within the government, he recognized the widespread doubts about Britain's ability to survive, particularly in the event of a German invasion, which was considered almost certain. When he looked across the Atlantic, he saw that the aid he so desperately needed was jeopardized by the growing belief in America that the British could not win.

In war as in electoral politics, people will rarely back the side that looks like a sure loser. When Churchill was worried about being abandoned by America, Murrow helped keep alive the idea that aid for Britain would not be wasted. Murrow's radio reports consistently depicted a determined England that could absorb any punch delivered by Hitler and fight back. Murrow's voice was crucial because, as Secretary of State Cordell Hull later wrote, "Had we had any doubt of Britain's determination to keep on fighting, we would not have taken the steps we did to get material aid to her."[68]

But some major players in the decision-making process did have doubts. Among the most important was the U.S. ambassador to Britain, Joseph P. Kennedy. Roosevelt had thought himself quite clever to have appointed an Irish-American to this job, but he had underestimated the turmoil that his aggressive, ambitious envoy could create. More comfortable with the brash gamesmanship of politics than with the nuances of diplomacy, Kennedy at first puzzled the British. He arrived in London in March 1938 and soon thereafter gave a speech about America's wariness of alliances. "In some quarters," he said, this caution "has been interpreted to mean that our country would not fight under any circumstances short of actual invasion." This, he said, was "a dangerous sort of misunderstanding to be current just now." His British audience liked that, but became somber as he continued: "Others seem to imagine that the United States could never remain neutral in the event a general war should unhappily break out."[69]

This ambiguity characterized Kennedy's tenure as ambassador. His biographer Richard Whalen wrote that "Kennedy resisted the use of U.S. influence to discourage war, which reduced the pursuit of peace to an ineffectual rhetorical exercise. An uncomprehending witness to the rise of new revolutionary forces, he could conceive of no conflict abroad that would affect vital American interests, no issue worth risking the lives of his or anyone else's sons." Further undercutting his effectiveness, Kennedy told a German diplomat that he intended to use all his influence to keep the U.S. out of war.[70]

Roosevelt did not want the United States to be perceived as tilting in any particular direction, and he especially did not want to provide implicit encouragement to Hitler. On Roosevelt's orders in 1938, Kennedy was told to remove a line from an upcoming speech that said, "I can't for the life of me understand why anyone would go to war to save the Czechs."[71] Soon after the war began, however, Kennedy changed his mind about the United States as arbitrator and sent a cable to the president urging him to intervene as peacemaker and "be the savior of the world."[72] But even that was a misstep by Kennedy. At that point such a move would have worked to Germany's advantage, and Secretary of State Hull told Kennedy that Roosevelt would undertake no initiative "that would consolidate or make possible survival of a regime of force and aggression."[73]

Despite the unhappiness he was causing in Washington, Kennedy did not back down. During a visit to Boston in late 1939, he told an audience, "There is no place in this fight for us." Response from the British press was swift. *The Spectator* noted that "there are plenty of eminent persons in the United States to give isolationist advice without the Ambassador to the Court of St. James's, who knows all our anxieties, all our ordeals, finding it necessary to join himself in that number."[74] In Whitehall, comments were more vehement. Foreign Office official Robert Vansittart, on learning of Kennedy's pronouncements in the United States, said the ambassador was "a very foul specimen of double-crosser and defeatist." Another Foreign Office official said Kennedy was "malevolent and pigeon-livered."[75]

When he returned to England in the spring of 1940, Kennedy remained pessimistic, publicly and privately. In a cable to the State Department, he said, "My impression of the situation here now is that it could not be worse." He reported a growing anti-Americanism in response to what was seen as U.S. foot-dragging about helping Britain, and said, "The majority of the English people feel America should be in this fight with the Allies," an opinion with which he strongly disagreed. He also told Washington policymakers: "Don't let anybody make any mistakes; this war, from Great Britain's point of view, is being conducted from now on with their eyes only on one place and that is the United States. Unless there is a miracle, they realize they haven't a chance in the long run."[76]

Although Roosevelt remained cautious about Britain's prospects, he did not want to rely on his ambassador's reports. On the same ship with Kennedy when he sailed back to Britain in 1940 was Bernard Baruch, traveling as Roosevelt's unofficial emissary. The president had sent him to talk with Churchill—at that point still leader-in-waiting—while Kennedy continued to deal with the fading Chamberlain.[77]

Kennedy's defeatist pronouncements reinforced the belief in Britain that Americans were ready to tolerate Hitler as a useful buffer against Bolshevism.[78] Roosevelt once said of Kennedy: "To him, the future of a small capitalistic class is safer under a Hitler than under a Churchill. This is subconscious on his part and he does not admit it."[79] Regardless of Kennedy's motivation, much of the U.S. public shared his pessimism; polls in the summer of 1940 found that only 30 percent of Americans thought England could win.[80] When Kennedy said that isolationist sentiment was growing in the United States "because the people understand the war less and less as they go along," the British press countered that the ambassador should have been doing a better job of explaining the conflict to his countrymen.[81]

Although British officials could not be certain how much impact Kennedy's pronouncements were having, they looked on the coverage provided by Murrow and other American journalists as a way to offset the ambassador's defeatist tone. Murrow went farther than that. He did not like Kennedy's slick charm or his close social ties to Britain's wealthy, particularly the "Cliveden set" that had strongly supported appeasement. When prominent British politician Harold Nicolson criticized the ambassador in an article in *The Spectator*, Murrow had a way to take a shot at Kennedy without doing so in his own words (which CBS would not have allowed). Murrow reported that Nicolson had written, "Were I to frequent only those circles in which Mr. Kennedy is so welcome a guest, I should also have long periods of gloom." Murrow went on to say that Kennedy's views would be welcomed by those who wanted to try to make a deal with Hitler: "the bankers, the knights and baronets, the shiver-sisters of Mayfair and the wobble-boys of Whitehall, says Mr. Nicolson." Then Murrow, having had enough of relying on "says Mr. Nicolson," added his own comment: "There is no doubt that a considerable number of people over here have resented Mr. Kennedy's utterances concerning the war. The British aren't accustomed to ambassadors expressing their frank opinions on international affairs in public. . . . American assistance and support, economic and moral, are welcomed in Britain, but advice as to how the war should be conducted or how the peace should be made is distinctly less welcome."[82]

The difference between Kennedy's and Murrow's opinions about the state of affairs was clear. The ambassador subscribed to the notion that Britain should save itself by accommodating Hitler, while Murrow—although far from optimistic—thought the British had a decent chance to survive if America provided aid. Murrow reported in late May 1940 that "many Britishers believe that these islands could be turned into a fortress off the coast of Europe, that it could hold out as long as the Navy is afloat and ships continue to arrive. Increased help from America is hoped for and expected."[83] That was the viewpoint of the Churchill government, and having it articulated by Murrow and delivered regularly to the American public and American policymakers was extremely useful.

Murrow did not, however, paint an unrealistically rosy picture of British prospects. When the German advance was roaring ahead in May 1940, he said that its speed "has staggered military experts here." He added that although there was no panic, "there is a feeling of surprise and bewilderment, a realization that the German bid for victory is directed by unorthodox minds, willing to attempt the impossible, and favored so far by incredible luck." A week later, he broadcast a description of British defenses being set up near the Channel coast in anticipation of a German invasion: "Buses, old cars, and trucks are parked all over the place, as though left there by drunken drivers, but when you look carefully you see there's not a spot where an airplane can land without plowing into an obstruction of some kind." He talked about his conversations with young RAF pilots, "the cream of the youth of Britain," who had just returned from fighting Germans in the skies above the beaches at Dunkirk. "There was no swagger about those boys in wrinkled and stained uniforms," said Murrow. "The movies do that sort of thing much more dramatically than it is in real life."[84] These images of quiet, determined heroism were the portraits of England that Murrow was sending to America almost every day.

※　　※　　※　　※

As British war planners monitored the journalism produced by Murrow and his colleagues, they recognized that it needed to be supplemented by a much larger flow of information into America. Murrow understood what was going on. "I believe Britain is about to increase her propaganda effort in the United States," he said in a broadcast at the end of May 1940, "and the attitude, as I've heard it, is this. 'The Americans think we're making propaganda anyway, so why shouldn't we do a better job of it?' The British believe they have a good case and a good cause and you can expect them to tell you more about it in the near future."[85]

By September 1940, the BBC was offering more than seventy news broadcasts each day—more than 200,000 words—to audiences outside the United Kingdom. Among the themes was that America had a stake in the war's outcome and that the British were "a first line of defense for the other side of the Atlantic." Commentator J. B. Priestley criticized the U.S. isolationists, saying, "All this patter about non-belligerence is like sitting down and doing crossword puzzles in front of a pack of ravening wolves."[86]

Murrow knew that radio enhanced the impact of propaganda: "If you believe that this war will be decided on the home front, then you must believe that radio used as an instrument of war is one of the most powerful weapons a nation possesses. If you believe, as I do, that this war is being fought for the control of men's minds, it is clear that radio will be a deciding factor."[87] Murrow was shrewd enough to know, as a corollary to this, that news reports such as his could be de facto propaganda.

Looking at it from another angle, propaganda could also have news value. Paul White wrote that CBS carefully monitored foreign programs through a listening center that recorded and transcribed between 100,000 and 150,000 words each day. He said that legitimate news items often turned up, and "the out-and-out propaganda broadcasts also supply news of another sort, since by one definition it is news if one learns what a combatant wants the other side and neutral nations to believe."[88]

Murrow privately offered advice to British officials who were reshaping the content of BBC broadcasts directed at America. He recommended using Americans on some of the BBC programs, and noted that although the U.S. audience for shortwave programs was small, it was largely made up of influential people and so would be worth targeting. Alfred Duff Cooper, appointed by Churchill to head the Ministry of Information, was receptive to Murrow's suggestion and the BBC no longer assumed that Canadians would be the sole North American audience for its overseas service.[89] In May 1940, the BBC began broadcasting "Britain Speaks," which brought the British worldview to U.S. listeners, and in September a "new and enlarged North American transmission" lasting six hours was inaugurated. The news, described as "a really reliable word picture of the very latest world events," was read with an American accent.[90]

As British information experts tried to devise strategies for influencing America, the Germans were well ahead of them. During the first weeks of the war, the Germans flew radio reporters to Poland, where the journalists were given a controlled, but firsthand, look at what was going on. In January 1940, Murrow arranged a double on-air interview: William Shirer in Berlin would talk with Ernest Udet, architect of the Luftwaffe, while Murrow in London questioned his British Royal Air Force counterpart. The British backed out, so Udet—who had completed a speaking tour in the United States—had the airtime to himself and was rewarded with follow-up coverage from the American press. Two months later, a similar episode: NBC interviewed Admiral Erich Raeder, commander in chief of the German fleet, about why neutral and unarmed ships were being attacked. U.S. networks offered the British Admiralty airtime to present its views on the matter, but the British again declined.[91] Even Hitler got American airtime. His speech to the Reichstag after the fall of France was carried by CBS. (The speech preempted the regular program in that timeslot, *The Goldbergs*).[92]

Some British officials recognized that they were being outmaneuvered by the Germans and that failing to cooperate with the news media was archaic self-indulgence. Roger Eckersley wrote, "It seems to me that the powers that be may not have sufficiently realized what part broadcasting can play in a war and that we are behind the Germans in this respect and that we cannot afford to rest on old tradition, but must play the enemy at his own game."[93]

The Germans also made heavy use of propaganda programs aimed at both British and American listeners. Beginning with his broadcasts from Germany in April 1939, Lord Haw-Haw (New York-born William Joyce) told British listeners every night that their government was corrupt and exploitive, representing only the upper classes that cared little for the needs of the mass public. He played on dissatisfaction with the Chamberlain government and it was estimated that half of Britain's eighteen million radios were tuned in to his broadcasts. Murrow noted that "each time he creates a doubt in the mind of a listener, he wins a victory. The British began by ridiculing him and are now taking him a little more seriously."[94]

When the blitzkrieg began, Joyce switched from preaching about social injustice in Britain to warning about military disaster awaiting the Allies. He told his listeners: "England is ripe for invasion. . . . You might as well expect help from an army of mastodons as from the United States. . . . Either England gives in before it is too late, or she will be beaten." He criticized Churchill, saying: "Perhaps if the British people could speak, they would ask for peace. But since the official voice of England asks not for peace but for destruction, it is destruction we must provide."[95]

By the time the phony war was over and Britain made ready to fight for its life, Lord Haw-Haw's appeal had run its course. Britons were listening instead to their new prime minister and so Joyce tried to recapture his audience by targeting America: "It stands to reason that the White House and Wall Street have only one fundamental interest in the rest of the struggle; namely, to induce the British to prolong it until Britain herself is so weakened that her possessions in the Western Hemisphere, including her capital investments, fall into American hands." With Germany on the attack, Joyce's speculation about U.S. intentions did not win back his British listeners.[96]

Meanwhile, Americans were also hearing from the Germans.

A German radio service for North America had been started in 1933, and as Hitler embarked on his course toward war the broadcasts praised isolationism, criticized Britain, and portrayed the new Germany in the best light, claiming, for example, that Hitler was simply trying "to straighten out some of the political and economic confusion with which Central and Eastern Europe were plagued."[97] Once the war began, this radio service sent America more than eleven hours of programming each day, including nine news programs and five commentaries, some from Lord Haw-Haw. Among the other broadcasters was Iowa native Fred Kaltenbach, who each week delivered an "open letter" that began, "Dear Harry and the folks back home in Iowa . . . ." In one of these letters, he warned his listeners about British propaganda: "The American people are to be led to believe that England and France are the last hopes of democracy, and that Germany is seeking to beat them only because they are democratic. Stuff and nonsense!" On another occasion Kaltenbach said, "Let it be said, once and for all, a German victory in this war is no threat to democracy—and certainly not to American democracy."[98] The broadcasts attempted to justify German policy to Americans by comparing the seizure of the Polish Corridor with the U.S. annexation of Texas, and likened Hitler's concept of *Lebensraum*—ensuring "living space" by controlling central Europe—to the Monroe Doctrine.[99]

The Germans' propaganda effort had a mission much different from that of their British counterparts. Substantial pro-British or at least anti-Nazi sentiment existed in America; a 1939 Gallup poll found that more than three-fourths of the American people wanted the Allies to win the war, while fewer than 2 percent favored a German victory. So the task for the Germans was not so much to win support as to help sustain isolationism. In one German newscast, the announcer said, "Above all, we cannot help congratulating the American people on their steadfast, neutral attitude . . . America *is* neutral. . . . She wants to stay neutral."[100] British Ministry of Information official Ronald Tree said the Germans had gone about their work ingeniously. "The two main themes," said Tree, "have been the injustice of the Versailles Treaty and that the war is merely a struggle for power between two imperialistic forces."[101] In other words, another European dispute (shades of 1918) best left to the Europeans to resolve. The Americans need not bother with it.

When American public opinion showed signs of shifting toward a stronger anti-Nazi outlook, the German broadcasts became more pointed. News-related skits tried anti-Semitic appeals, using as their negative characters "Mr. Finkelstein" and "Mr. Rosenbloom." In his broadcasts, Kaltenbach complained about Americans being influenced by anti-German propaganda. "The German government and the German people," he said, "have left nothing undone to court American favor. And how has this been rewarded? With reproaches and rebuffs. . . . It is not too late, however, to extend the hand of friendship to the strongest power in Europe."[102]

American self-interest was stressed frequently in the German broadcasts, and German-Americans were warned about being victimized by the spreading anti-German feeling: "Don't let it get you down, you German-Americans. . . . People whose opinions really count will admire you for sticking up for Germany in a fight which is no concern of the United States." Once France was out of the war, the German theme became more stridently anti-British: "England is standing on her last legs. She stands all alone in Europe and there is nothing the United States can do to stave off her defeat at the hands of Germany. And why should she want to? What has England ever done for America?" Similarly: "The fight for a lost cause may be thoroughly honorable in itself," but "it hardly behooves a young, vigorous nation like the United States to stand in the way of progress and the New Order."[103] One of the German commentators argued that "there is a far greater similarity between American democracy and German National Socialism than there is between old-fashioned English class distinction and Americanism."[104]

On any given day in early 1941, the American audience for the German broadcasts was estimated at about 150,000, but there is no evidence that the German radio efforts accomplished anything beyond feeding the gospel according to Goebbels to the small number of Nazi sympathizers in America.[105] If the Nazis' programs created any drag on the pro-British drift in American opinion, it didn't amount to much.

The German radio campaigns directed at Britain and America were, however, an interesting example of the use of broadcasting as an intellectual weapon. Murrow understood what propaganda was designed to do. "The real objective of broadcasting into enemy countries," he said, "is to hack away at civilian morale, undermine the will to fight, create doubts as to the honesty and integrity of national leaders, emphasize and exaggerate social and economic inequalities, boast of your own achievements while pointing out that the enemy is without hope and fights for an unworthy cause."[106]

As governments came to better understand the political power of radio, they struggled to control it. Control could be exercised almost reflexively—if not always wisely—through censorship. Part of the motivation for censoring news was to protect security interests; part was to avoid diplomatic and other political problems. For instance, when Murrow traveled to the still-neutral Netherlands in January 1940, Dutch officials strictly censored his reports because they did not want to provoke the Germans.[107]

Sometimes de facto censorship occurred inadvertently. At the beginning of the war, British inexperience in dealing with radio journalism was evident. When the British Expeditionary Force was making ready to go to France, of the fifty slots for journalists only two were allocated for American radio reporters, although there were three major networks. CBS reporter Bill Henry, for one, had to wait six weeks while his paperwork moved through the bureaucracy before he was allowed to catch up with the BEF.[108]

More formal British censorship policy was to require a written script for all broadcasts—no ad-libbing. A censor, or "scrutineer," was always on duty at the BBC's facility, following the script while listening to Murrow or whoever else was on the air. CBS executive Paul White said the British censorship was "on the whole a friendly one." Reporters in Germany, however, faced a more difficult process. White wrote that "in Berlin the correspondent's script must pass a triple censorship by the military, diplomatic, and propaganda ministry's representatives. Severity of censorship in the German capital varies widely and for no apparent reason. At times the American radio men have found their copy so badly decimated by blue pencil that they have simply refused to broadcast." He added that the journalists gradually became adept at self-censorship; they "learned what the authorities consider information 'of aid and comfort to the enemy,' such as weather reports and precise descriptions of aerial bombing damage," and so left such material out of their scripts.[109]

As British officials worked out their censorship plans, they recognized that Murrow and his colleagues needed reasonable freedom of movement if they were to provide coverage that accurately reflected life in Britain at war. In late spring 1940, American journalists were given Scotland Yard passes that allowed them to move freely throughout London, and the Ministry of Home Security expedited clearance for visits elsewhere in the country.[110] Equilibrium was established as more British officials came to understand that American news coverage was not a nuisance that needed to be controlled but rather could be a crucial asset in nudging the United States toward providing meaningful assistance.

❋ ❋ ❋ ❋

Roosevelt, meanwhile, was performing a complicated juggling act. His principal political business centered on engineering his campaign for a third term in the White House. Until the summer's Democratic Convention, he refused to publicly make a decision about running again, keeping politicians of both parties in suspense, but his policymaking was grounded in the political necessities of a reelection race. Concerning Europe, he had no illusions about Hitler but knew he might jeopardize his election chances if he came to Britain's aid in a way that seemed to be pulling America closer to entering the war. Recognizing this, Churchill told Chamberlain in early 1940 that Roosevelt "is our best friend, but I expect he wants to be reelected and I fear that isolationism is the winning ticket."[111]

Roosevelt understood that eventually America's place would be alongside Britain but he intended to move in that direction with great care. To that end he continued to dispatch emissaries to size up the situation in England—whether the British really could hold out against the Germans and whether Churchill was someone he wanted as a discreet partner if American support was to be quietly provided. In early 1940, he sent Undersecretary of State Sumner Welles to Germany, France, Britain, and Italy to determine if there was any chance for achieving a permanent peace. (He told Welles that he had no interest in a flimsy armed truce.) Welles was unable to push any of the countries toward an agreement, but he was impressed by British resolve. In Britain, he later wrote, "one could sense a determination that they would fight to the last ditch to make it impossible for Hitler to force them to do his bidding." The British, said Welles, would see the war "through to the end no matter how far off that end might be, nor how bitter the progress toward it might prove."[112]

Several days after becoming prime minister, Churchill pressed Roosevelt for help. In a cable, he wrote: "I trust you realize, Mr. President, that the voice and force of the United States may count for nothing if they are withheld too long. You may have a completely subjugated Nazified Europe established with astonishing swiftness, and the weight may be more than we can bear."[113] Churchill then presented a wish-list that included everything from antiaircraft ammunition to specific positioning of the American fleet. Roosevelt, with the election less than six months away, agreed only to bits and pieces of Churchill's requests. The prime minister replied to Roosevelt that "we are determined to persevere to the very end" and told Ambassador Kennedy that even if the Germans overran Britain, "the Government will move to Canada and take the fleet and fight on."[114]

Roosevelt was not convinced, despite Churchill's courage, that

Britain could survive, and he found little encouragement for sub-stantively aiding the British in American public opinion polls, which consistently reflected a desire to avoid even the periphery of the war. When the British ambassador, Lord Lothian, asked Roosevelt to warn Germany that the United States would intervene rather than allow Britain to be defeated, Roosevelt was sympa-thetic but he told Lothian such a move was politically impractical. He estimated that he could get just 40 percent of the public and 25 percent of the Congress to support such a declaration, and if he followed that course prior to November he would ensure election of an even more isolationist Congress.[115]

Recognizing that the cautious Roosevelt needed to be pushed gently, Churchill relied on radio to make his country's case di-rectly to Americans. His rumbling rhetoric encouraged the Ameri-can public to maintain faith in Britain's determination to carry on. Eleanor Roosevelt later said that his speeches "were a tonic to us here in the United States as well as to his own people."[116] In some ways, Churchill and Murrow were proceeding on parallel paths, using the airwaves with consummate skill to nudge their listeners toward a desired political viewpoint.

No other politician before Churchill had so effectively used the combination of rhetorical eloquence and radio's international reach. In his speech in the House of Commons following the Dunkirk evacuation, the prime minister admitted that "wars are not won by evacuations," but said "we shall prove ourselves once again able to defend our island home, to ride out the storm of war, and to outlive the menace of tyranny, if necessary for years, if necessary alone." He continued, "We shall defend our island, whatever the cost may be, we shall fight on the beaches, we shall fight on the landing grounds, we shall fight in the fields and in the streets, we shall fight in the hills; we shall never surrender." Although that passage is the most quoted excerpt from that speech, what followed was more significant in terms of acknowl-edging Britain's new standing in the world. The balance of glo-bal power had changed, with England's destiny now in America's hands. And so, said Churchill, Britain "would carry on the struggle until in God's good time the New World, with all its power and might, steps forth to the rescue and the liberation of the Old."[117]

Murrow described the speech in his broadcast that night: "There were no frills or tricks. Winston Churchill's speeches have been prophetic. He has talked and written of the German danger for years. He has gone into the political wilderness in defense of his ideas. Today, as prime minister, he gave the House of Commons a report remarkable for its honesty, inspiration, and gravity."[118] Murrow consistently presented Churchill to Americans that way—a fierce and articulate leader who was worth helping.

While Churchill pursued his courtship of Roosevelt, America's reluctance to take a firm stand in opposition to Germany was causing British patience to wear thin, particularly because even buying war supplies was becoming more difficult. Foreign Office official Alexander Cadogan said of the situation: "What it seems to amount to is this: that at any given moment we shall run out of dollars. We may then, with the possibly small chance of success, have to throw ourselves on the mercy of the Americans."[119]

Murrow reported that among England's political leaders, the increasingly prevalent attitude was "those who are not for us are against us," and his broadcasts in mid-1940 took on a tone of greater urgency, particularly after the French gave up the fight. The feeling among the British, he said, was that "in the old days, a war could be lost—a few colonies or provinces ceded to the enemy—and the vanquished people could then begin to prepare for the next time. These people are pretty well convinced there won't be any next time if this war is lost." He said that his friend Harold Laski, a noted political theorist, had told him, "We fight till we win, or we die." He noted that the British press was offering advice to Americans, with the *Daily Express* warning the United States not to follow the British course after Munich: "We breathed a sigh of relief and sank gently into a complacency that now astounds and humiliates us. . . . America, don't be English. Don't accept the soft words of reassurance that come from Germany." Murrow also cited the *Daily Herald*, which said, "For Americans' own sake, we fervently trust that they too will not be lulled until almost too late by the wishful nightmare of appeasement and the slogans of splendid isolation."[120]

Murrow may have argued that he was just a messenger carrying the words of the English press, but his selection of newspaper passages such as these conveyed his own message to America. Some of his British colleagues believed there was more to his reporting than simply covering events. Thomas Barman, who left his job as a reporter for the *Times* of London to join the British government's Enemy Propaganda Department, later said: "What else were his broadcasts designed to do but stimulate American public opinion on the side of the British Isles? He must have had that in mind." BBC producer Mary Adams said, "He believed in the cause. . . . Others wanted a good story."[121] Some in Britain tapped into Murrow's knowledge of American politics; one visitor came to the Murrows' apartment to ask who might be the best emissary to approach the U.S. pro-intervention groups for help in getting more military material for Britain, especially ammunition.[122]

CBS correspondent Charles Collingwood said that Murrow always told his listeners when he was offering his personal opinion. "There was nothing sneaky," said Collingwood, "about the way he got his opinion through."[123] An example of this was a Murrow broadcast in July 1940: "Occasionally, in reporting this war, the reporter is obliged to express his personal opinion, his own evaluation of the mass of confusing and contradictory statements, communiqués, speeches by statesmen, and personal interviews. It has always seemed to me that such statements of personal opinion should be frankly labeled as such without any attempt to cloak one's own impressions or opinions in an aura of omnipotence. What I think of events in Europe is no more important than what you think, but I do have certain opportunities for observation and study."[124]

Despite his disclaimer in that broadcast, Murrow's opinions could be found in many of his reports without being "frankly labeled as such." Because he was seen by many as being on the "right side," he was not often challenged about violating standards of journalistic objectivity. After all, he was just reporting what he saw. But those who wanted America to stay out of the war recognized that Murrow's broadcasts, although they did not overtly endorse intervention, constituted a powerful brief for American action. Murrow kept one step back from the edge of explicitly calling for the United States to go to war and that apparent reticence kept most listeners from dismissing him as a proselytizer. His audience had, after all, been hearing from the likes of Father Coughlin, Adolf Hitler, and an array of others who brought a "hot" presence to radio (to use a term that Marshall McLuhan would apply to television several decades later). Murrow was a "cool" practitioner, which made him more welcome in listeners' homes and enhanced his influence.

❋   ❋   ❋   ❋

Murrow may have leaned toward interpretive reporting as opposed to just reciting facts partly because he was frustrated by radio's time constraints. In a letter to a friend in New York, he voiced a complaint similar to those frequently heard from later generations of broadcast journalists: "I gnash my teeth over this business of doing four- or five-minute spots from here, which means one must deal really with headline stuff. There's no opportunity to talk about the fundamental things that are happening, the things which cast a shadow over future happenings at home." In another letter, he said, "The news has now been completely prostituted."[125]

Throughout his career, Murrow was a resolute champion of high journalistic standards. He also understood the relationship between technique and effect—how "good radio" (and later "good television") enhanced the basics of journalism. Beyond the process of news, he respected the power that journalists could wield. Soon after his arrival in Britain, he had given a speech at the Royal Institute for International Affairs in which he noted that "international broadcasting in one sense seems to me to have become altogether too conscious of its dignity. There is too much the feeling that a man speaking to another country suddenly takes on the status and responsibilities of an ambassador. Under certain conditions, the voice of an English cab driver or fisherman may do more to influence American public opinion than a learned discourse by one of your outstanding scholars." He underscored the need for responsibility: "Until the search for truth and its diffusion to listeners becomes the main objective of international broadcasting, radio will not assume its proper significance for modern civilization. . . . It has enormous power, but it has no character, no conscience of its own. It reflects the hatreds, the jealousies, and ambitions of those men and governments that control it. It can become a powerful force for mutual understanding between nations, but not until we have made it so."[126]

Eighteen years later, Murrow would make similar comments about the unfulfilled potential of television. But in 1940, he just wanted radio to become more responsive to the public's need for truth.

❈   ❈   ❈   ❈

During that summer, Britons heard little good news. Their country was standing alone as Hitler tightened his domination of the rest of Western Europe. In the United States, *Time* summarized the American mood: "If U.S. public opinion last week could be gauged in a sentence, it was this: Hitler was invincible in Europe, Britain was facing probable defeat, the U.S. had best look to its own security." The article cited a *Fortune* magazine poll that found 94 percent of respondents in favor of spending "whatever is necessary" to strengthen the U.S. military.[127]

Nevertheless, as Churchill wrote, "the buoyant and imperturbable temper of Britain . . . may well have turned the scale." The British people, he said, "were not even dismayed. They defied the conquerors of Europe. They seemed willing to have their island reduced to a shambles rather than give in."[128]

Fears of invasion remained paramount. The Germans planned their move into England based on the assumption that they could first destroy the Royal Air Force, but the British had an advantage over the vaunted Luftwaffe: the fastest fighter in the world, the Vickers Supermarine Spitfire, which could fly at 362 mph and could climb to 11,000 feet in just under five minutes. In addition to the Spitfire, the British had the Hawker Hurricane, which could fly at 328 mph.[129] Relying on these two aircraft, the RAF would prove during the Battle of Britain that it would not be destroyed.

By the beginning of September 1940, the war had been underway for a year. "Europe has suffered much this last twelve months," said Murrow. "The next year and the years after that will twist and torture minds and bodies. Reporting Europe will not be a pleasant task."[130] London was now being bombed with devastating effect, and Murrow visited Londoners in their shelters: "How long these people will stand up to this sort of thing, I don't know, but tonight they're magnificent. I've seen them, talked with them, and I know."[131]

This was just the beginning of London's ordeal. The relentless fury of the blitz would soon arrive and Londoners would have to stand up to much more. Murrow would be standing there with them to tell their story.

Chapter 2

Murrow's England

When we think of Ed Murrow today, we tend to remember the craggy face and cigarette-roughened voice that we know from his television years. But when he sailed for England in 1937 to run CBS's European operations, he was just twenty-eight years old, youthful in outlook as well as appearance.

With him was his wife Janet, whom he had married in October 1934. Two years younger than Ed, she threw herself into building their English life. She also kept in touch with home, writing long, detailed letters sometimes several times a week. She typed many of them and began them "Dear families," making a carbon copy so the same letter could be sent to her parents, Charles and Jennie Brewster, and Ed's parents, Roscoe and Ethel Murrow. She tried to alternate who got the original and who got the carbon, but at one point she told her parents that she usually sent them the carbon because she couldn't remember who was supposed to get the original, and "I'm less afraid of offending you than the Murrows." The letters are wonderfully written and convey what it was like to live in London during that time of nervous excitement, when war was still a distant menace.

Ed quickly set up shop in the London CBS office at 14 Langham Place, and he and Janet settled into their flat at 49 Queen Anne Street, inherited from Ed's CBS predecessor, Cesar Saerchinger. Janet reported in mid-summer that their boxes of books had arrived from America, but "of all the tragedies the piano couldn't be gotten up the stairs," so it was sent back to a warehouse. Among her early feelings about London was regret that the home of poets Robert and Elizabeth Barrett Browning on nearby Wimpole Street had been torn down. She also noted how polite the London policemen were to her. The Murrows explored the city on long Sunday walks and took in some grand events, such as George VI's coronation procession. They went to Wimbledon to see Don Budge and Alice Marble play tennis and came back, said Janet, "determined to play a beautiful game the next afternoon." But the inspiration of Wimbledon could lift the level of their game only so far: "We went over to Regent's Park and never played more horribly in all our lives. It was a terribly hot day and we just couldn't get them over the net."

They also plunged into London's cultural life. One evening they were taken by a friend to the ballet and dinner at the Savoy. Janet told the families that "the ballet was really lovely and even Ed enjoyed it, which he hadn't hoped to do." Ed was not always so well disposed toward the arts. When they finally got around to seeing *Gone With the Wind,* reported Janet, "Ed kept saying, 'God, this is horrible,' in all the most sentimental parts, much to the annoyance of the people about us."

Janet was also meeting people, such as the Archbishop of York, who, she said, "in his gay red togs, his hands folded over his fat tummy, laughing a laugh that shakes him all over, looks for all the world like a jovial keeper of a country pub."[1]

They traveled beyond London, spending country weekends with the Saerchingers in Surrey and with political theorist Harold Laski, an old friend of Ed's, in Essex. Some of her letters reflect a twinge of homesickness, as when she told of making a weekend trip "north of London to Colchester and Ipswich and back through the country roads. There's more color in the trees in the country, though they never get as bright as they do at home."

Some of the traveling was less pleasant. Janet wrote of staying in "a horrible hotel in Dover—most English hotels are horrible and fairly dirty." But that was the exception. Ed and Janet were enjoying the good life of pre-war Europe: theater parties and late-night suppers in London; quick visits to Paris with dinners at Maxim's and the Ritz. On one trip to Paris, they dined with Murrow's CBS colleague Bill Shirer and Janet reported that during the course of the meal "I think I learned how to make Crepes Suzettes."[2]

During summer 1937, while Ed worked, Janet went to Nice, France, for a short stay. Ed's letters to her are those of the young husband, not the journalist: "Each time I'm away from you the sense of how much I love you and depend on you deepens," he wrote. And: "It's really hot in London. I've been wandering about this town at night like a lost soul in Hades. . . . Never before have I missed you so much. . . . The more I think of it the smarter I think it is that you should see something of Europe while you can. Later on, even if we don't have any money, we'll have a few memories. . . . It seems ages since you left and I want to see you so much."[3]

Dark clouds, however, were gathering over the Murrows' work and pleasure. In early 1938, when Janet wrote that they were looking for a new flat, she also noted that "Nobody seems to know what Mr. Hitler is up to." The following April, she wrote home excitedly about finding a Sheraton highboy that she could get for $80 at an antique market, but said she would not purchase this chest of drawers "until after Hitler's speech on the 28th. If things bid fair to be quiet until autumn—and maybe later—as we think they will, I think I shall buy it." She ended up not buying it, deterred by the growing possibility that things would not be quiet through the autumn. Ed was less cautious. Even after the war was underway and London was being pounded, he occasionally bought expensive pieces of antique silver that caught his fancy.[4]

As war drew nearer, CBS executives in New York demanded more stories, and the European staff found itself hard-pressed to keep up. Janet volunteered to help out, and did occasional broadcasts about Easter services at Westminster Abbey and other home-front items. After one of her early efforts, she asked her family: "What did you think of me as a broadcaster? . . . I thought a lot about it before I wrote the thing, and it may interest you to know that I wrote every bit of it myself. I was thrilled to think that Ed didn't change any of it. . . . Ed was pleased and so was New York, and I think I'll be able to help out now and then with feature stuff." After she had done a few more, she wrote: "I've liked doing them and hope to do some more. I don't get paid for them, but I'm glad to free Ed from having to write one now and then." Ed used her work often enough that he wrote to the Tottenham Court Road police station in 1940 to request that Janet be exempted from curfew regulations, asking "if you would extend to Mrs. Murrow the privilege of staying out after midnight as I would like her to do some broadcasting to America on our late night program which occurs at midnight."[5]

In the spring of 1940, when the war was going badly, the Murrows made up their minds that they both would remain in England. Janet wrote, "We decided a year ago that the only thing to do was to live dangerously and not run away from things." When they made that decision, during the war's early days, they were trying to adjust their lives to new dangers. Janet had written in her diary in September 1939, "Couldn't make myself take gas mask out when went to do errands," and in a letter home, she said, "I'm not afraid of being bombed." As the strangeness of wartime was starting to take hold, she asked her parents: "Is it really autumn in America? Are the kids going back to college? Do you go to horse races and amuse yourself? It certainly seems years ago that we planned to do anything just for fun. There's nothing at all to do in London. At seven o'clock up go the black paper linings for the windows."[6]

As the months passed and phony war became blitzkrieg, Janet tried to reassure the Brewsters and Murrows, although, she admitted, "the conflict seems on our very doorstep." "I know you're worried and probably frantic," she wrote, but "please don't be. . . . What I want you to know is that life goes on very normally here. We eat and sleep and go about our business. I don't pretend for a moment that I'm going to be brave when bombs start bursting about me—if they do—but I don't think about it any more than I have to." She could not, however, push all her concerns aside. She told the families: "Ed will be going off to the coast and other hot spots to see what can be seen—in order to tell you about it. I hate to have him go off, not because I mind staying alone but because I feel it is so dangerous. I don't worry about it because that's no good, but I don't rejoice either."[7]

When Ed was in London, Janet often waited alone for him in their new flat on Hallam Street. He would not get home from the BBC headquarters a few blocks away until well after midnight. Janet told her parents that Mary Street, an older woman who lived in a flat below the Murrows, had "heard that my husband was out all night broadcasting. So, thinking I'd be nervous if there were air raids at night, she wanted me to know that she'd be glad to have me come down at anytime and sit with her. She has made a gas-proof room out of one of her small rooms. I thought it was terribly sweet of her to say I might share her gas-proof room." Janet reported that Miss Street had also told her she'd be ready at any hour: "I'm an old trouper. When I hears the guns I tuck me nightie in me knickers and put on me shoes."[8]

Some nights, Janet had plenty of company. With many wives and children having left London for safer places, "our flat has become sort of a gathering place. Around our fireplace, you'll find from one to ten newspaper correspondents, broadcasters, members of Parliament, or 'hush-hush' people who belong to one or another of the Government departments. I'm kept busy providing food and drink for all of them and listening as hard as I can to their words of wisdom. You'd be surprised how screwy some of them are."

During her days, wrote Janet, "I run errands, sometimes type my husband's scripts, do an occasional broadcast of my own, chauffeur people about while they search for broadcasting material." She also helped the American Committee for the Evacuation of Children, although she lamented that mostly the wealthier families were able to send their children to the United States and "the ones who ought most to go are the ones who because of lack of money will be left behind."[9]

Janet's principal work was as head of the London office of Bundles for Britain, which was formed in late 1940 to administer private American aid efforts. During its first six months, women in 1,100 Bundles branches in the United States sent 250,000 knitted garments, 500,000 other pieces of clothing, seventy-two mobile feeding units, and more than two million dollars. The money went for such things as $10,000 worth of replacement equipment for Royal Crest Hospital after it was bombed. At one point, Bundles was raising money to help seventeen bomb-damaged hospitals in London. Janet later toured the industrial English Midlands and reported on the needs of those who had been bombed out of their homes there. She presented a mobile canteen donated by people from Spokane, Washington, to a hard-hit London borough and occasionally did broadcasts for CBS describing Bundles projects. The aid provided by Bundles for Britain did not match the amounts sent by the American Red Cross, but Bundles had American women in London working with the British, and that hands-on presence helped to improve Britons' opinion of Americans.[10]

That was important, given British concern about America's refusal to enter the war. In one letter home, Janet told about a woman on a London bus asking her how she liked London in wartime. "Before the conversation ended, she said very pleasantly, 'Mind you, I think this should be your fight as well as ours.'" Janet was increasingly of that opinion herself. In her diary in March 1940, she dismissed Undersecretary of State Sumner Welles's "peacemaking" mission as "a rank political move on the part of Roosevelt," and she added, "Growing opinion America yellow."[11] At about the same time, *New Yorker* writer Mollie Painter-Downes reported that "perhaps it's worth recording that the British attitude toward the hope of American intervention is now one of weary but complete resignation to the belief that in this war the Yanks will not be coming."[12]

Although there was growing disdain in England for the American government, Ed's political clout with the U.S. public was increasingly recognized in Britain and by Americans coming to take a look at wartime London. The Murrow flat in the unassuming brick building became an ever more popular gathering place, and over the years visitors such as Eleanor Roosevelt and Clark Gable turned up, as did British political figures including Ernest Bevin and Harold Laski. Diplomats, journalists, and others who had been chased out of various parts of Europe also came by. Jan Masaryk, foreign minister of the Czechoslovakian government-in-exile, became a close enough friend that he didn't need to wait for a dinner invitation, and would frequently stop in. He made himself at home, and if Ed, who had a low regard for Brussels sprouts, left some on his plate, Masaryk would say, "You can't do that," and spear them for himself.[13]

Sometimes, dinner was elsewhere, as when Murrow arranged a party at the Savoy for British friends to meet American writer Alexander Woollcott. Murrow—occasionally accompanied by the young CBS correspondent Eric Sevareid—also spent evenings at Laski's home where the talk was often about the inequities of the British class system.[14]

※　　※　　※　　※

Despite his critical comments about the British social structure at Laski's gatherings and occasionally on the air, Murrow had, according to journalist Ernie Pyle, "a terrifically wide acquaintanceship among the English-who-matter."[15] Invitations from the social elite flowed to the Murrows: Lady Rhondda asking them to dinner at The Ivy restaurant; Lord Strabolgi wanting Ed to set aside an evening for dinner and political discussion; the Countess of Listowel wishing they would join her at her home for dinner. As the pace of the war quickened and Murrow's workload expanded, most of these invitations were politely turned down.

The Murrows did, however, find time for some friendships that gave them a close look at the upper echelons of British life and afforded them some welcome weekend escapes. They occasionally visited Great Wigsell in East Sussex, the home of Lady Violet Milner, widow of former foreign secretary Lord Salisbury and more recently widow of Alfred Viscount Milner. Lady Milner

followed news of the war avidly, and wrote to Murrow in summer 1940 to say that she had been told by an American acquain-
tance that CBS broadcasts from Europe reflected pro-German
sympathies. Murrow quickly responded, "I am convinced that
this is not, and never has been, the case with broadcasts from
London." On another occasion, he sent Lady Milner, at her request, a copy of one of his broadcast scripts.[16]

Lady Milner introduced the Murrows to Sir Edward and Lady
Grigg, who invited Ed and Janet to their home in Gloucestershire.
While there, Janet went to tea at the home of Lady Grigg's mother,
Lady Islington, whose house had been built in the time of William and Mary and had its own deer park. In a letter home, Janet
wrote, "I thought I'd seen lovely houses before, but hers takes
the prize."[17]

Other friends included Lady Milner's nephew, Lord Cranborne (who became the Marquess of Salisbury) and his wife, Elizabeth, who were known as "Bobbety and Betty." One Murrow admirer was Lady Reading, who said that Ed possessed "the three
qualities that every Englishman treasures above all others and
wants for his son—absolutely fearless, had some ethical values,
and was very generous."[18] As their social contacts proved,
Murrow's dislike of the British class system did not translate into
aloofness. He and Janet enjoyed the comforts they were invited
to share with the wealthy, just as Ed liked buying his suits from
exclusive Savile Row tailors.

Even many of the Murrows' untitled friends were wealthy
and owned impressive country homes. David Keir had a grand
house in Kent and nominated Ed for membership in the Savile
Club. Janet visited Dorothy Darvall, wife of Ministry of Information official Frank Darvall, in Cumberland and wrote that her
hosts "own all this beautiful sheep country as far as the eye can
see." Another Ministry of Information official with whom the
Murrows became close was Ivison MacAdam and his American
wife Carolyn, described by Janet in a letter as "a Corbett from
Portland, Oregon. Her family is an old lumber family. Very
wealthy." Early in the war, the MacAdams had sent their two

young children to Carolyn's family in America, and Janet reported that Carolyn "misses the children dreadfully, but doesn't dare go to them [because] she might not be able to get back." On Christmas Day 1939, Murrow arranged a live CBS audio hookup so Ivison and Carolyn could speak to their children in America.[19]

On numerous occasions, Murrow provided British friends with help that was more substantive than setting up a radio connection. He wrote to friends in the United States asking that they serve as guarantors for people applying for American visas, which was required by American law. On occasion, Murrow promised that he would be "responsible for any financial support they may require while in the States," as he assisted Ministry of Information officials and others in sending their families out of the war zone to the safe haven of America.[20]

The most notable of the Murrows' friends were Winston and Clementine Churchill. Mrs. Churchill was the honorary sponsor of Bundles for Britain, and came to know Janet through that organization. In a letter home, Janet wrote: "Mrs. Churchill came to inspect our new office. We all talked for about an hour and off she went. The office is only around the corner from Downing Street, so Mrs. Churchill walked home. She's really lovely, so pretty and very vivacious." Six weeks later, Janet reported to her mother, "Mrs. Churchill asked me to tea the other afternoon."[21]

There were more Downing Street invitations. Once when Ed came to pick up Janet after her lunch with Mrs. Churchill, the prime minister heard his voice and came out of his study: "Good to see you, Mr. Murrow. Have you time for several whiskies?" Churchill understood how Murrow and other American journalists might influence U.S. opinion, but Janet later said that the relationship between the two men was cordial but never became particularly close: "Churchill was too bound up in himself to be seeking out the advice of an American journalist. He was fond of Ed, and Ed, of course, worshipped him." Contact between the two men increased after America entered the war, and Ministry of Information official Ronald Tree later wrote that Murrow enjoyed "the friendship and complete confidence of Churchill."[22]

In all these relationships—from the weekends at Lady Milner's country house to the dinners at 10 Downing Street—Murrow grew closer to the England he was covering. Some of the Murrows' British friends were more conscious than others about the importance of courting Ed Murrow. They recognized that the tone as well as substance of his reporting could affect the American public's sympathy for the British cause. Churchill might become exasperated with Roosevelt's caution about providing aid, but he too was a politician and he understood why the American president wanted a cushion of supportive public opinion when undertaking a politically risky enterprise. Murrow, with his large and attentive audience, could help provide that cushion, and so reinforcing this American's affection for Britain and the British was important.

Murrow never gave any indication that he thought his friendships were undermining his objectivity. If there was a political purpose behind his reporting, it was a desire to let the world know about the evil of Hitler's Germany. If he could help that be fully recognized, American policy would, perhaps, shift. As for his socializing with those whom, in a broad sense, he was covering, he could make the case that the drawing rooms of London mansions and country estates were the true centers of British policymaking and proper territory for a journalist's visits. Among the most famous of the grand homes where politics flourished was Cliveden, the Berkshire estate of Nancy and Waldorf Astor.

❊   ❊   ❊   ❊

Nancy Astor was an American who became the first female member of the House of Commons. Her husband Waldorf Astor, also an American, was the great-grandson of John Jacob Astor and was reckoned to be one of the world's wealthiest men. When they married in 1906, she became the chatelaine of Cliveden, a grand Italianate house overlooking the Thames not far from Windsor, which had been built in the late seventeenth century and was purchased by Astor in 1893. When she learned of the sale, Queen Victoria lamented that the historic property should now belong to an American: "It is grievous to think of it falling into these hands."[23]

After Nancy was elected to Parliament in 1919, her house parties at Cliveden and at their London home at 4 St. James's Square took on more of a political flavor (although not an alcoholic one; she favored total abstention and served nothing stronger than ginger beer and cider). By the mid-1930s, she had become politically devoted to Neville Chamberlain, who was a frequent guest at Cliveden. Among other influential visitors were Geoffrey Dawson, editor of *The Times,* Barrington Ward, chief editorial writer of *The Times,* and J. L. Garvin, editor of *The Observer.* The Astor family owned *The Times* and *The Observer,* and both papers supported Chamberlain's approach to dealing with Germany.[24]

Nancy laid out her own position on appeasement in a May 1937 speech to a Conservative Party meeting in her constituency. She argued for an "Anglo-German pact," noting that mankind "did not live in a world of angels" and so needed to find expedient ways to maintain peace.[25] With her close ties to the prime minister and others, Nancy was thought by some to wield great influence on British foreign policy, an idea that was popularized by Claud Cockburn in his left-wing publication *The Week.* In November 1937, Cockburn published a report about negotiations purportedly going on between Britain and Germany that would give Hitler a free hand in Central Europe in exchange for Germany making no colonial claims elsewhere for the next ten years. Cockburn wrote that the proposal had been designed by "the queer Anglo-American" gathering at Cliveden that "exercised so powerful an influence on the course of 'British' policy." He claimed to know of "pro-Nazi intrigues centering on Cliveden and Printing House Square [*The Times* office]."[26]

Cockburn's reporting was flawed; he said the pro-appeasement Lord Halifax was part of the gathering, but he wasn't there, and he overlooked the presence at Cliveden of Anthony Eden, who was a leader of the anti-appeasement forces. Nevertheless,

Cockburn's notion of a foreign policy cabal was picked up and amplified by other publications. The weekly *Reynolds News* was the first to use the term "the Cliveden Set," and Cockburn himself started using it the following month. Newspaper items referred to "Schloss Cliveden" and cartoonist David Low depicted "The Shiver Sisters"—Nancy Astor, editors Geoffrey Dawson and J. L. Garvin, and diplomat Lord Lothian—dancing to a gramophone under the motto "Any sort of peace at any sort of price," with Goebbels as dancing master. Even *Time and Tide* magazine, which was edited by Nancy Astor's friend Lady Rhondda, published an article titled "Clivedenism" that seemed to agree with the conspiracy theory.[27] Murrow looked on the Cliveden crowd with the distaste he had for anyone who embraced appeasement.

Cockburn took pride in his creation, claiming that "no anti-fascist rally in Madison Square Garden or Trafalgar Square was complete without a denunciation of the Cliveden Set." He said that members of the group were "friends of the Third Reich" and that Halifax had made a trip to Germany not on an official government mission but "as the representative rather of Cliveden and Printing House Square." Most of this was nonsense, but it was repeated often enough to find a place in the public's and policymakers' conversation. Harold Nicolson wrote in his diary, "How terrible has been the influence of the Cliveden Set," which "prevented us from taking a strong line while it could have made for peace." Anthony Eden, traveling in the United States, wrote that "Nancy and her Cliveden Set have done much damage" with the result that most Conservative Party members were viewed as "fascists in disguise."[28]

Nancy Astor was not adroit at damage control, as shown by her choice of guests. She invited Joachim von Ribbentrop, when he was serving as Germany's ambassador to Britain, to one of her other homes (although he never came to Cliveden). High-profile figures considered to be pro-German, such as Charles Lindbergh, visited both Cliveden and the Astor house on St. James's Square. Lindbergh preached his gospel of the superiority of German air power to all who would listen, and one of his most attentive disciples at the Astors' salon was Joseph Kennedy, who proceeded to tout Lindbergh's views to officials in London and Washington.

Lady Astor also gave luncheons at her London home that brought politicians and journalists together. One that she organized for Neville Chamberlain and American reporters backfired when the journalists reported that the prime minister had discussed—without first briefing the House of Commons—an idea for an alliance among Britain, France, Germany, and Italy that would eventually be aimed at the Soviet Union. She dug an even deeper hole for herself during a 1937 visit to America when she decried "the appalling anti-German propaganda here" and said, "If the Jews are behind it, they've gone too far and it will react on them." Not surprisingly, such comments fueled opinion that she was pro-Hitler. One fellow member of the House of Commons referred to her as "the honorable member for Berlin."[29]

From Washington, British Ambassador Lord Lothian wrote to Nancy: "The Cliveden Set yarn is still going strong everywhere here. It symbolizes the impression spread by the Left and acceptable to the average American that aristocrats and financiers are selling out democracy in Spain and Czechoslovakia because they want to preserve their own property and privileges . . . and Chamberlain is their tool."[30]

Some of the Astors' friends did their best to debunk the Cliveden Set stories. Sir Henry "Chips" Channon, another American-born member of parliament, disputed the "talk of a 'Cliveden' set which is alleged to be pro-Hitler, but which, in reality, is only pro-Chamberlain and pro-sense." Whitehall official Tom Jones, a frequent Cliveden visitor, wrote that "such was the variety and individuality of the persons gathered together that the notion of their forming a Cliveden Set was as grotesque as it would be to expect unity among the passengers of a Cunarder" passenger liner. He added that Cliveden was "an unplanned setting for informed talk, a comfortable theater for the conversational interplay of political personalities." Along similar lines, George Bernard Shaw wrote an article for the American magazine *Liberty*, which had carried a story linking Charles Lindbergh to Cliveden. Shaw noted that although you might meet Lindbergh at Cliveden, you could also encounter strong anti-fascists such as Charlie Chaplin. Of the whole Cliveden Set theory, said Shaw, "Never has a more senseless fable got into the headlines."[31]

Although vilified as a Hitler sympathizer in many of the Cliveden Set stories, Nancy Astor sometimes used her influence to challenge the Germans. In 1938, Felix Frankfurter, soon to become a U.S. Supreme Court justice, asked Nancy for help in locating his uncle, an elderly professor who was among the many Viennese Jews arrested by the Germans after they annexed Austria. Rather than going through British diplomatic channels, Nancy went directly to German officials. She wrote to Frankfurter: "Dear Friend, The minute I received your wire I spoke to the German ambassador in London and gave him, in no uncertain terms, our views on arresting aged scholars. He promised to do what he could. Three days afterward, having heard no more, I talked to him again and warned him that unless I received good news of Herr Frankfurter, I would go myself to Vienna! He assured me that it would be alright. As you know, your uncle was released on the 28th March."[32]

By May 1940, Nancy realized that appeasement had failed and that her dear friend Chamberlain needed to be replaced. She joined the group of forty Conservatives who voted with Labor against the Government, precipitating Chamberlain's resignation. She said of Chamberlain, "No man did better for peace, but he was hopeless for war."[33]

The Cliveden Set existed in the sense that influential people—many of whom were politically like-minded—often visited the Astors' estate. But there is virtually no evidence to support the notion that participants in these social gatherings were concocting and implementing a privatized British foreign policy that involved making secret deals with Germany. Publications such as Cockburn's *The Week* were the political equivalents of today's celebrity-fixated tabloids, and the Astors and their friends were fine fodder for readers ready to distrust the rich and powerful.

To a certain extent, Murrow bought into the Cliveden Set story. Like Churchill, he believed that envisioning coexistence with the Nazis was foolhardy. He was particularly averse to Joseph Kennedy's view—popular among Nancy Astor's coterie—that Britain could not survive unless it made a deal with Hitler. Murrow agreed with his friend Harold Nicolson, who in an article for *The Spectator* said that Kennedy was welcomed in England only by "the peace-pledge union, the friends of Herr von Ribbentrop, and members of former pro-Nazi organizations."[34] Murrow quoted Nicolson's article approvingly during a spring 1940 broadcast, and he remained impatient with those on both sides of the Atlantic who, in his judgment, refused to acknowledge the reality of the German threat. When he cited Nicolson or other opponents of appeasement and depicted the British debate about dealings with Germany in terms of good versus evil, Murrow sent a clear signal to his listeners about where he stood.

❀   ❀   ❀   ❀

While criticizing those who gathered at Cliveden, Murrow kept company with his own set, primarily advocates of American intervention, many of whom were engaged in the British government's efforts to influence U.S. public opinion. Among the closest to Murrow was Ronald Lambert Tree.

Ronnie Tree was born in England to American parents. His father was the Oxford-educated son of a Chicago family and his mother was the daughter of department store founder Marshall Field. He studied on both sides of the Atlantic, including a stint at the Columbia University Journalism School. He married the niece of Nancy Astor, and the couple settled in England. One of their homes was Ditchley, a 4,000-acre Oxfordshire estate that Janet Murrow described as something between "a palace and a country club."[35] In late 1940, Churchill asked Tree if he might stay at Ditchley on weekends "when the moon is high." Apparently, the Germans had taken aerial photographs of the prime minister's official country residence, Chequers, and had dropped bombs nearby. British military officials worried that Churchill would be vulnerable at Chequers, particularly on moonlit nights when the German bombers were most active and had a good view of targets. Tree agreed, of course, and hosted the prime minister frequently throughout the war.[36]

Tree was elected to parliament as a Conservative in 1933. A back-bencher who opposed Chamberlain's appeasement policy and supported Anthony Eden, he was part of a small group that in early 1938 "started meeting together in an effort to put pressure on the Government to accelerate rearmament, set up a Ministry of Supply, and substitute Churchill and Eden for some of the more defeatist of the older members of the Cabinet." A few months later, said Tree, after the Munich agreement "this Edenite group became an active entity," and its members were promptly dubbed "warmongers" by Chamberlain supporters. During one party at Ditchley, Tree and Nancy Astor argued, with Tree supporting Eden and Lady Astor championing Chamberlain. "We went at it hammer and tongs," wrote Tree. The government took such opposition seriously; Tree later learned that as a result of his activities, his phone had been tapped.[37]

Because of his personal history and professional interests, Tree was considered one of the relatively few experts on America in the British government. Eden asked Tree to accompany him to America in late 1938 to help him with speaking appearances and meetings with the press. In January 1940, Tree was asked to join the Ministry of Information, with special responsibilities in its American division. Tree later noted that "at this time, lack of knowledge of the United States in Government and political circles was abysmal." He added that "towards America amongst the older men in the Cabinet there was a feeling of distaste mingled with irritation. We were at war, the Americans were not."[38] Despite these feelings, the British leadership knew that the United States must be wooed. An internal Foreign Office memorandum cited the importance of "cultivating the good graces of powerful sections of American public opinion, on whose good will we are in the last analysis dependent for victory."[39]

Murrow and Tree became friends soon after Murrow came to England. "We shared a mutual dislike of Mr. Chamberlain," wrote Tree, "and during those Munich days he used to come see me in the House of Commons for a talk and a drink." (Later Tree was among the Conservatives who voted against Chamberlain on the crucial May 1940 no-confidence measure.) The Trees and the Murrows also found time to socialize. "From the early days of the war," said Tree, Ed and Janet "were constant visitors to Ditchley. There was nothing that made him happier than a day in the fields with my keeper, a gun, and a dog, and coming back with a brace of partridge and a pheasant or two."[40]

Tree was also a bridge between Murrow and the Ministry of Information (MoI). Headquartered in the Senate House of the University of London, MoI was notably ineffective in its pre-Churchill incarnation in terms of its impact on American public opinion. This was principally because Foreign Office officials and the British ambassador to the United States, Lord Lothian, limited the ministry's efforts due to fear that anything perceived as propaganda would backfire, playing into hands of isolationists who argued that Britain was trying to entice the United States into war. Lothian wrote to a friend in early 1940 that Britain was "drifting into difficult waters" in its relationship with the United States, particularly with regard to what Americans perceived as British propaganda. Lothian's view was shared by others who thought that it would be better to let Americans such as Murrow engage in de facto propagandizing for British interests.[41]

Tree agreed with Lothian but he understood journalism well enough to know that providing plenty of information, not merely cajoling reporters, was the best way to get helpful coverage. His position was that the MoI "should see that all the facts about the war are made available as quickly as possible to the American correspondents. They are extremely friendly to us and they can be relied upon to see that our side of the case is put forward, always providing that it is given accurately and quickly to them."[42]

But Tree also understood American political sensitivities

about propaganda. In the U.S. Senate Foreign Relations Committee, Missouri Democrat Champ Clark had introduced a resolution calling for "a full and complete investigation of the activities of any person, firm, or corporation acting for any nation, by way of propaganda or otherwise, having as their ultimate goal of tending to cause, directly or indirectly, a change in the neutral position of the United States in the conflicts now being waged abroad."[43]

Tree later wrote that the American Division of MoI "was in the stultifying hands" of Sir Frederick Whyte, who took the "no propaganda" mandate so seriously that little was done beyond serving as a clipping service—sending stories from the British press to America and noting stories about Britain in U.S. publications. In September 1940, Whyte was replaced by journalist Douglas Williams and the MoI became more enterprising. At the top of the ministry, Sir John Reith was replaced by Alfred Duff Cooper, who had contributed to the *New York Herald Tribune* and had spent time in America on a lecture tour. He had also been war secretary and first lord of the admiralty, and so he had some idea of how to manage military information. Duff Cooper plodded along for about a year before being replaced by Brendan Bracken, who was one of Churchill's top aides, had been managing director of *The Economist* and chairman of *The Financial News*, and knew something about America.[44] Many of these architects of Britain's information efforts, such as Duff Cooper and Bracken, were frequently Tree's guests at Ditchley, as was Murrow.

Bracken turned out to be the most effective leader of the MoI. He had become close to Churchill during the days when the future prime minister was dismissed by many as a bellicose fool, and, trying to reinforce the image of closeness, Bracken did not discourage rumors that he was Churchill's illegitimate son. John Colville, Churchill's private secretary, described Bracken this way: "Underneath a mop of wiry, uncontrolled red hair, behind thick glasses and a pretended ruthlessness, lay a heart of gold; and he had a memory so remarkable, for people, events, and the architecture of houses, that when Brendan was available no books of reference were required. In the years immediately before the war, and during the war itself, he was a bright comet sweeping across the skies, afraid of nobody, jolting Churchill out of melancholy or intemperate moods, and proving a strikingly successful Minister of Information, in contrast to his three predecessors in the post."[45]

When Churchill's friends were in short supply, Bracken wrote, "No public man in our time has shown more foresight, and I believe that his long, lonely struggle to expose the dangers of dictatorships will prove to be the best chapter in his crowded life."[46] Bracken was also an admirer of Murrow and praised him as "the most faithful friend of Britain" who had "made friends here who will never forget what he did for us."[47] After the U.S. had entered the war, Bracken—with Churchill's approval—offered Murrow the job of running the BBC's news programming. Murrow seriously considered the offer, and during a visit home consulted, among others, Justice Felix Frankfurter, who urged him to accept the position as a gesture of wartime solidarity. But Murrow, fearing the dilemmas that would arise from divided loyalties, turned Bracken down.[48]

Until Bracken's arrival, the MoI had not accomplished much, disseminating mostly bland "information" rather than hard news that would interest journalists. In early 1941, Tree was sent to America to set up a British Information Service that would provide usable material to U.S. news organizations. The new venture, said Tree, was designed to ensure "that the American people could be given the fullest picture of Britain's all-out effort, and so they could clearly understand that nothing short of total defeat, which now appeared remote, would change her unswerving resolve to continue fighting until victory had been achieved." When Tree asked Churchill about what approach to take in the information effort, the prime minister said he should stress the threat of Hitler gaining control of all of North Africa, which, along with submarine warfare, would let the Germans dominate much of the South Atlantic and so provide them a relatively easy hop across to Brazil. "In my opinion," said Churchill, "there would be little resistance shown in the countries of South America to Nazism. Once established in South America, they would be able to move up to Panama and Central America, and this would constitute a grave threat to the United States. It is this that I would advise you to ram home to them in every possible way."[49]

After a six-week visit to the United States, Tree recommended a full-scale public diplomacy program: British spokesmen to come to America to talk about the life of a country at war, with particular attention paid to winning over the mostly isolationist U.S. working class; contacts to be established with universities and the larger intellectual community; Americans to be brought to England for a first-hand look; information bureaus to operate in the Midwest and on the West Coast, as well as in New York. Eventually most of Tree's recommendations were adopted, but even then differences of opinion remained. For instance, Tree commissioned a documentary to be made for U.S. audiences to show how American donations were helping Britain. Tree was pleased with this thank-you on film and he screened it for Churchill, expecting him to like it as well. Instead, Churchill ordered that it not be sent to the United States, saying, "It will merely encourage them to think that they can get away with gifts."[50]

Meanwhile in Washington, Ambassador Lothian, despite his fastidiousness about "propaganda," was having considerable success in his dealings with American journalists. He was approachable and reporters found that he would not consciously mislead them. He persistently made the case that America was endangering itself by not aiding Britain, and when asked how the United States could help, his standard reply was, "Give us your old destroyers." Lothian made careful judgments about which journalists he could trust and he provided confidential information to some, such as John L. Balderston, a former *New York World* London correspondent, who published a pro-intervention newsletter that he sent to about fifty important U.S. newspapers.[51]

Lothian believed that his missionary work was productive, but he recognized that winning over America remained a delicate process, with the word "alliance" requiring particularly sensitive use. In a letter to Nancy Astor in early September 1940, he wrote: "Public opinion is moving so fast towards recognizing that cooperation with England is essential to American defense that while there will be a row in Congress, I don't think there will be serious trouble. But tell people in England not to talk about an Anglo-American alliance. That always means entanglement in Europe to U.S.A. Strengthening the defense of both is a better line."[52]

Churchill was among those in London who avidly scrutinized diplomatic and journalistic reports from America. He particularly liked the lively dispatches from Isaiah Berlin, a young political philosopher who was working at the British embassy in Washington. Later in the war, when Churchill heard that Berlin was in London, he wanted him to come to lunch so he could quiz him about American politics. The invitation, however, was mistakenly sent to *Irving* Berlin—the songwriter—who also happened to be in London. He happily appeared for lunch and was asked about goings on in America, but his responses did not satisfy Churchill, who did not know which Berlin he was talking to. When he found out about the mix-up, Churchill said, "I thought he was not so forthcoming as his dispatches."[53]

❋   ❋   ❋   ❋

Churchill and his colleagues in government were primarily concerned not about the reports they received from Washington, but rather the flow of information from Britain to America. As American journalist Vincent Sheean described it, "the zeal with which London people, particularly those in political and governmental circles, welcomed the American correspondents in 1940 was an index to their true sense of the situation. They might not talk about it frankly, but in their innermost consciousness they were sure that the war could not be won by England alone. America was tardy, reluctant; the American correspondents had the ear of America; therefore American correspondents were to be flattered, courted, made much of."[54]

Murrow was in the first rank of these American correspondents, and British information officials kept abreast of his status within CBS. In early 1940, a memo circulating within the BBC noted that Sinclair Refining Company would begin sponsoring Murrow's *European Roundup* broadcast, which was the first time CBS had agreed to have direct commercial sponsorship of the news program (a foreshadowing of news as a network profit center). Several days later, Murrow sent a note to the BBC's Roger Eckersley assuring him that "this action involves no change whatsoever in either the content or editorial control of the broadcast." Eckersley told others at the BBC that the sponsorship was a "great compliment to Murrow." Others at the BBC saw how selective sponsorship might influence content of other broadcasts, and one official suggested that the Ministry of Information, "through its agents in America, arrange for some sponsoring firm to take on a weekly commentary of the Raymond Gram Swing type from this country to New York."[55]

Murrow was not alone in being valued by the British. Sheean said that among the American journalists, "Quent Reynolds was the one who most touched the British imagination, seemed the most American and at the same time the most solidly a friend. I think many English people saw in him . . . a sort of promise of American participation in the war. His tributes to English courage and perseverance, expressed without reserve, delighted a people which had some distaste for self-praise and yet knew that it had deserved it well: he said what they did not quite like to say themselves."[56]

Reynolds gathered information for his stories everywhere from the high-toned Savoy Hotel bar to the bomb-battered streets. He liked anecdotes and personality sketches, recognizing that people are interested in other people, so to win and hold an audience he would discuss even the most complicated political issues in terms of how they affected individuals. In his articles for *Collier's* and the books he turned out rapidly, he wrote about London and Londoners. "I never knew," he wrote, "that people were so wonderful. Taxicab drivers, waiters, charwomen, waitresses, actresses—even wealthy West Enders who I thought would crack first—all take their beating each night, shake the noise of the night from their heads, and face the new day and its dangers with calmness." He also wrote that "London is more alive tonight than it has ever been in its history. . . . London is fighting for its existence. London can never die as long as the spirit of London lives. No bomb, no land mine has yet been devised which is capable of killing this spirit."[57]

In Reynolds's London diary, which was published as a book in 1941, he spoke of the frustrations that many American journalists in Britain felt. He wrote: "If it is important to America that England win the war, it is about time that America began to help. . . . England is fighting with her back to the wall, all right. It is rather humiliating to watch her fight a war that is ours just as much as it is hers." Another entry: "I've done my best to be an objective reporter as regards the war. I think I've managed to be objective in my *Collier's* articles. But it is hard to be objective when you see your friends murdered."[58] This was the kind of comment British officials loved to see.

Murrow's outlook was similar to that of Reynolds, but his role was more significant. In addition to influencing American opinion through his own broadcasts, Murrow helped shape the way that Britain presented itself to the United States. Murrow's colleague Eric Sevareid wrote that "Murrow was not trying to 'sell' the British cause to America; he was trying to explain the universal human cause of men who were showing a noble face to the world. In so doing he made the British and their behavior human and thus compelling to his countrymen at home." But there was more to it than that. Godfrey Talbot of the BBC said that Murrow had "an inordinate admiration for what Britain was like in those days, and he was concerned, very concerned, that his own country wasn't aware of the facts of life, and that if Hitler and Co. were not stopped here, the next stop was Manhattan."[59]

So Murrow did more than just broadcast for CBS. When he advised the BBC to broaden the target audience of their North America shortwave broadcasts to include Americans as well as

Canadians, the heavy mail response to the BBC's New York office after the initial broadcasts indicated that he had been right. The BBC then asked Murrow to suggest an adviser to help shape the content of their North American broadcasts, and he recommended journalist Wells Church.[60] The first BBC North American Service broadcast with a U.S. emphasis aired in May 1940. Presenter Vernon Bartlett said: "I am going to talk to you three times a week from a country that is fighting for its life. Inevitably, I'm going to be called by that terrifying word 'propagandist.' But of course I'm a propagandist. Passionately I want my ideas—our ideas—of freedom and justice to survive." Among the special features of this new America-oriented programming were "Answering You," which addressed questions sent in by American listeners; "Listening Post," which analyzed German radio propaganda; and "The Stones Cry Out," about historic English buildings destroyed by the Nazis.[61]

Murrow was a frequent guest on the North American Service program *Freedom Forum*, which discussed political issues, and he served as the chair when regular moderator Sir Frederick Whyte was not available. Murrow also started his own series for the BBC, *Meet Uncle Sam*, which included analysts such as American historian Allan Nevins and the British-born Alistair Cooke, who remained a commentator on American affairs into the twenty-first century. Murrow also advised the BBC about its plans for broadcasting into occupied France, offering suggestions about how to train the French broadcasters and urging that the programs avoid personal attacks on Marshal Henri Philippe Pétain, head of the Vichy government, for fear that such an approach would alienate those in France who might not like Pétain but did not want him criticized by outsiders.[62]

Murrow also participated behind the scenes in British efforts to establish a listening center that would analyze foreign radio broadcasts' effectiveness as propaganda. The stated purpose of the study was to determine "the extent to which broadcasting was being used . . . to influence public opinion in its attitude toward foreign affairs, and also the extent to which the domestic government-controlled broadcasts on international affairs in the totalitarian states gave an indication of the line which their policies were likely to follow." An early version of the plan called for the listening operation to be run by the London CBS office, with Murrow directing the listening staff's selection of broadcasts and administering grants (including some CBS money) that would fund the project.

In the terminology of today's intelligence community, this would fall within the category of "sigint," or signals intelligence. When it was implemented in the spring of 1939 it was a quasi-intelligence operation pushed along by people with ties to the British security services and the Foreign Office. As it finally developed, the project was begun not as an adjunct to CBS but under the auspices of the Royal Institute of International Affairs (RIIA). Murrow remained closely involved, and minutes of an RIIA meeting identified him as the person "through whom the proposed analysis of broadcasts had come before the Royal Institute." Other documents indicate that Murrow served as the go-between linking the RIIA and the Rockefeller Foundation, which provided the money for the startup. (Later, during the Cold War, the Rockefeller Foundation allegedly was used on occasion as a CIA funding conduit.[63]) Once the project was up and running, Murrow visited the listening center's original site. Shortly before the war began, the operation was transferred to the BBC.[64]

When considering Murrow's involvement in such extracurricular projects, a purist ethical argument could be made that a journalist should not be so closely involved with the subject of his coverage—in this case, the British war effort—and should not serve even informally as an adviser to policymakers, particularly those of a foreign—albeit friendly—government. The counterargument, implicit in Murrow's actions, is that ethical flexibility is necessary when the stakes are so high.

Despite Murrow's claims that he was an objective observer, the top British leadership assumed that he was not neutral. The low-profile help he provided in London, plus reports from the British embassy in Washington about the impact of his broadcasts, led to Murrow being seen as a valuable asset by Churchill and other officials.[65]

In trying to awaken America, Murrow was on the side of the "good guys." Perhaps that gave him ethical leeway.

❀   ❀   ❀   ❀

While Murrow was becoming more involved with British efforts, Franklin Roosevelt was approaching the moment when he had to make up his mind about providing the aid that Churchill so persistently sought. In July 1940, Roosevelt sent William Donovan to England as his personal envoy to once again appraise Britain's chances of survival. Donovan was a Republican with a distinguished record of service in World War I, and he later became the head of the Office of Strategic Services, the predecessor of the CIA. His independence was respected by American politicians and policymakers, and the importance of his visit was recognized by top British officials, including William Stephenson, a senior British intelligence operative based in New York. Stephenson later said that at the time of Donovan's mission, "the United States government was debating two alternative courses of action. One was to endeavor to keep Britain in the war by supplying her with material assistance of which she was desperately in need; the other was to give Britain up for lost and to concentrate exclusively on American rearmament to offset the German threat."[66] Stephenson recognized that Donovan's findings could tilt the debate's outcome one way or the other and so he urged British authorities to fully cooperate with their visitor.

Concerned that Joseph Kennedy would pound home his pessimistic predictions and color Donovan's findings, Roosevelt did not inform the U.S. Embassy that Donovan was coming (which greatly irritated Kennedy when he eventually found out about it). During his two-week visit, Donovan worked on his own, meeting with King George, Churchill, British military leaders, and many others. He asked Ronald Tree to help him get detailed information about the supply situation and, with Churchill's blessing, Tree quickly assembled a comprehensive report. Before returning home, Donovan told U.S. military attaché Raymond Lee that he estimated the odds at 60-40 in favor of the British fighting off the Germans.[67] Back in the United States, Donovan delivered his upbeat message to the president, cabinet members, and members of Congress, giving Roosevelt a useful assist in re-shaping American aid policy.

In August 1940, Attorney General Robert Jackson provided Roosevelt with a formal opinion that a deal to provide Britain with fifty destroyers in exchange for leases on British territory in the Western hemisphere could be legally implemented without asking the consent of Congress.[68] In November, Roosevelt won re-election, defeating Wendell Willkie by five million votes and a substantial Electoral College margin. A month later, the president justified the lend-lease approach to reporters, saying, "There is absolutely no doubt in the mind of a very overwhelming number of Americans that the best immediate defense of the United States is the success of Great Britain defending itself."[69] At least some of the aid that Britain so badly needed would soon be on its way.

❋   ❋   ❋   ❋

Meanwhile, London was absorbing a terrible pounding from the Luftwaffe. Murrow reported that Londoners were adjusting their lives. "No longer do we hear the sound of church bells on Sunday morning," said Murrow. "They will be rung only to announce the arrival of air-borne [German] troops. There were no seaside holidays for Londoners this year. The beaches are being reserved and prepared for fighting." He added that Londoners "have become more human, less formal. There's almost a small-town atmosphere about the place. . . . There's been a drawing together."

Some Americans living in London joined in, at least symbolically, forming a Mobile Defense Unit that was affiliated with the Home Guard. Its members were armed with weapons imported privately from the United States, and were commanded by a veteran of the Spanish-American war. The unit performed guard duty at London public buildings until it stood down in 1944.[70]

Despite such gestures, Murrow was impatient with most of his countrymen. He cloaked his frustration in dispassionate rhetoric, as when he told his listeners that as a reporter in the midst of Britain's courageous efforts, "one feels very small and humble. We can only continue to give you the news and the atmosphere in which it happens. You must reach your own conclusions."[71]

As he said that, the Battle of Britain was underway, with the British proving their courage in the skies and in the streets of their battered cities.

---------------------------- Chapter **3** ----------------------------

London Besieged

On the afternoon of September 7, 1940, nearly a thousand German planes—348 bombers escorted by 617 fighters—darkened the skies over London. After a two-hour attack, another wave arrived. The principal targets were the docks along the Thames, and the Ministry of Home Security reported that 430 persons were killed and 1,600 were badly injured.[1] This was Adolf Hitler's version of shock and awe.

For the next fifty-seven nights, London was hit again and again. For a while, the bombers came by day as well, but the Royal Air Force destroyed so many German planes in the sunshine that by mid-October a daytime attack was a rarity. When darkness fell, however, London was blasted.

At this time, the population of Greater London was about eight million. (New York was then seven million.) Only one other city in the United Kingdom—Glasgow—had more than a million people. With about one-fifth of the entire population of Britain located within 750 square miles, the London area was an obvious target once Hitler had decided—unwisely, as it would turn out—that he would rather try to break Britain's spirit than destroy its RAF bases.[2] The German press said the raids were aimed not only at military and economic targets, but also at "British arrogance, the boundless conceit of Lords and Gentlemen."[3]

But the main motive behind the bombing, which also did much damage to cities such as Coventry and Plymouth, was to soften up Britain for an invasion, Operation Sea Lion. In order for Germany to mount its cross-Channel assault before bad weather set in, the Luftwaffe had to cripple both the RAF and the British willingness to fight by late September. Otherwise, the invasion would have to be postponed.

London had been heavily bombed earlier; one notably destructive raid had come in late August. It was the relentlessness of the blitz that set it apart—night after night for two months. Afterwards there were more raids, less predictable in their timing but no less ferocious, that continued until May 1941. Later in the war there would be still more attacks on London, most devastatingly by V-1 flying bombs and V-2 rockets in 1944 and early 1945, but the blitz was the real test of Britain's ability to stand alone and survive.

An estimated 20,000 tons of high explosives were dropped on London within nine months. Watching the results one night, journalist Vincent Sheean wrote: "The flames seemed to spread far beyond the unseen horizon, into the farthest reaches of the dark. . . . It was like a vision of the end of the world."[4] Eric Sevareid wrote that on the first day of the blitz he saw "terror in the eyes of hundreds as they moved in great migration away from the awesome pillars of black oil smoke, trudging through snowpiles of powdered glass, pushing their prams, heads turned over shoulders, staring eyes fixed upon the quiet and mocking sky."[5]

Six years earlier, George Bernard Shaw had peered gloomily into the future of warfare and predicted that "great fleets of bombing planes over capital cities will cause them to raise the white flag immediately rather than suffer destruction."[6] He was wrong. Instead the attacks on London led Britons to stiffen their resolve and proved, said Sheean, "the ability of the great city and its people to stand severe punishment, the resolution of the Churchill government to fight to the last, the inability of the German air force alone to win the war."[7] *Time* magazine observed that "Britons had dug down to the marrow of each British bone and to the ganglion of each British nerve" to demonstrate that they could fight.[8]

For the first few days, the working-class East End took the

brunt of the attacks. If that had kept up, social unrest might have begun to boil as the poor suffered while the rich watched. But on September 13, the Germans targeted Buckingham Palace. The king and queen escaped unhurt but the attack underscored that this was everyone's war.

The breadth of the devastation was stunning. During the first six weeks of the blitz, 16,000 London houses were destroyed, 60,000 were seriously damaged, and 300,000 people needed temporary housing. One Londoner in six was homeless at some point during the nine months of the blitz.[9] The world had never seen anything like this use of massive air power against civilians.

For Americans, "it has nothing to do with us" remained the prevailing sentiment as the blitz began. They were still spectators, intent on keeping their distance. Radio, however, narrowed that distance. Murrow, determined that his countrymen would not ignore battered Britain, brought the war into their living rooms with vivid and sometimes poetic descriptions of what was going on around him. He told them that on the first day of the blitz "the fires up the river had turned the moon blood red. The smoke had drifted down until it formed a canopy over the Thames; the guns were working all around us, the bursts looking like fireflies in a southern summer night." He reflected Londoners' scorn for the enemy; the bombing, he said, "makes headlines, kills people, and smashes property, but it doesn't win wars. . . .Things will have to get much worse before anyone here is likely to consider it too much to bear."[10]

Londoners' toughness was a theme that ran through many of Murrow's broadcasts. He said: "I've seen some horrible sights in this city during these days and nights, but not once have I heard man, woman, or child suggest that Britain should throw in her hand. These people are angry."[11]

Virtually all of Murrow's broadcasts gave his listeners a good sense of what it was like to be in the midst of the blitz. In one report he spoke of what he had seen during "several hours of observation from a rooftop" while the bombing was underway, and in another he said: "The air raid is still on. I shall speak rather softly, because three or four people are sleeping on mattresses on the floor of this studio." He told of the resolve of firefighters, police officers, railroad workers, and others who combed rubble for the dead and the still living and dealt with unexploded bombs. "Military medals," said Murrow, "are getting rather meaningless in this war. So many acts of heroism are being performed by men who were just doing their daily job."

He also noted little things. He described the "rainbow bending over the battered and smoking East End just when the 'all-clear' sounded." He told of standing in front of a smashed grocery store and hearing a dripping inside. He investigated and found that "two cans of peaches had been drilled clean through by flying glass and the juice was dripping down onto the floor." And in the background there were symbols of resilience and continuity: "The tolling of Big Ben can be heard in the intervals of the gunfire." He was trying, he said, to give a sense of "the life in London these days—the courage of the people; the flash and roar of the guns rolling down streets where much of the history of the English-speaking world has been made." But, he added, "these things must be experienced to be understood."[12]

Implicit in such references to "the history of the English-speaking world" was a reminder to Americans of their kinship with Britain. This was not just another country in dire straits, too "foreign" to worry about; this was America's parent. Murrow wanted to inspire some family loyalty.

By September 21, Murrow had convinced British authorities to allow him to broadcast live from a rooftop while the bombing was going on. He painted pictures with his words while the war provided the soundtrack: "Four searchlights reach up, disappear in the light of a three-quarter moon. . . . Just overhead now the burst of the antiaircraft fire. . . . The searchlights now are feeling almost directly overhead. Now you'll hear two bursts a little nearer in a moment. There they are! That hard stony sound." The next night: "I'm standing again tonight on a rooftop looking out over London, feeling rather large and lonesome. . . . As I look out across the miles and miles of rooftops and chimney pots, some of those dirty-gray fronts of the buildings look almost snow white in the moonlight here tonight." He saw a rooftop spotter and said, "There are hundreds and hundreds of men like that standing on rooftops in London tonight watching for fire bombs, waiting to see what comes out of this steel-blue sky."[13]

That kind of reporting underscored the difference between broadcast and print. Although a newspaper reporter could eloquently write about this same scene, there was something special about the mix of voice and background sounds arriving in faraway homes. The impact of this was heightened by its novelty; the world had not yet become accustomed to real-time news delivering the sounds (and, later, sights) of every major story as a matter of course. For the American audience, secure in its isolated cocoon, these reports stirred imagination and, perhaps, conscience.

The German Propaganda Ministry was also listening to Murrow and seized upon one of his observations to try to portray British resolve as crumbling. He had said: "Presumably plans for the evacuation of London have been ready for more than a year, but I do not believe that serious consideration is being given to such a step at the moment. The King and government still are in London, and unless it becomes untenable I believe they will remain." The Germans claimed that Murrow's mention of evacuation plans had meant that the royal household and government were preparing to leave. Murrow, through the British Ministry of Information, denounced the Germans' misrepresentation of his reporting.[14]

Murrow's CBS colleagues reported other facets of London life. Eric Sevareid described the pace of early evening when Londoners knew that darkness would bring the bombers: "People walk rapidly. They glance at their watches. If they stop to buy a paper, they stuff it in their pocket and hurry on. They run for darkened buses or stand in the middle of the street, impatiently whistling for taxis that go speeding by. Mothers are walking rapidly, pushing baby buggies, looking at the sky and thinking they're hearing a siren each time a car starts up in second gear."

When Sevareid left Britain in October to return to the United States, he delivered a farewell that echoed Murrow's sentiments: "Paris died like a beautiful woman in a coma, without struggle, without knowing or even asking why. One left Paris with a feeling almost of relief. London one leaves with regret. Of all the great cities of Europe, London alone behaves with pride and battered but stubborn dignity. . . . London fights down her fears every night, takes her blows and gets up again every morning. You feel yourself an embattled member of this embattled corps. The attraction of courage is irresistible."[15]

Evocations of British courage helped offset the defeatists' predictions that England would not survive. But survival was being bought at an excruciating price. Even when the nighttime attacks became more sporadic, tremendous damage was done to London. After the bombing on December 29, 1940, more than 1,500 fires raged, most in London's ancient heart, the City. St. Paul's Cathedral, built after the Great Fire of 1666, survived, even though it was hit by twenty-eight incendiaries. One of these lodged in the outer shell of the dome, beyond reach of any firefighting equipment, and began to melt the lead. But before the dome went up in flames, the device fell onto the parapet and sputtered out. Perhaps the worst raids occurred the following April 16 and 19: more than a thousand Londoners were killed each night and 148,000 houses sustained some damage. In these strikes, the Germans used JU88 dive bombers, which added to the terror as they screamed downward in their attacks.[16]

Despite the death and destruction they were able to cause, the Germans never attained their goal of weakening Britain to the point at which an invasion would be likely to succeed. On October 12, 1940, after a month of intensive bombing, Hitler's headquarters issued this directive: "The Fuehrer has decided that from now until the spring, preparations for 'Sea Lion' shall be continued solely for the purpose of maintaining political and military pressure on England. Should the invasion be reconsidered in the spring or early summer of 1941, orders for a renewal of operational readiness will be issued later."[17] Hitler had lost the

Battle of Britain. As he turned his eyes eastward toward Russia, the prospect of invading England faded away.

Meanwhile, Churchill saluted the RAF airmen who "undaunted by odds, unwearied in their constant challenge and mortal danger, are turning the tide of the world war by their prowess and by their devotion. Never in the field of human conflict was so much owed by so many to so few."

❋   ❋   ❋   ❋

While Britain fought, Murrow worked, sometimes broadcasting four or five times a night after walking the London streets to survey the damage the Germans had done in their most recent raid. He wouldn't rely on government press releases; he had to see things for himself and he always wanted a better, closer view. When the Air Ministry at first blocked his efforts to do live broadcasts from rooftops with a view of the city, he appealed to Churchill, who "approved heartily" and overruled the military bureaucrats. There was an informal partnership between Murrow and Churchill. The prime minister had been a journalist in his younger years, and he appreciated Murrow's talent and resolve. Above all, he recognized that the more leeway Murrow was granted to do his reporting the more likely that he could rouse American sympathy.

Murrow's colleague Elmer Davis said: "The only objection that can be offered to Murrow's technique of reporting is that when an air raid is on he has the habit of going out on the roof to see what is happening, or of driving around town in an open car to see what has been hit. That is a good way to get the news, but perhaps not the best way to make sure that you will go on getting it."[18] Vincent Sheean said that Murrow's "courage, endurance, and obliviousness to fatigue made it possible for him to survive many months of a cruel schedule. He could go without sleep as long as might be necessary, broadcasting at all sorts of hours and working like a slave between times. His courage was of the kind I most respect: that is, it did not consist in lack of sensitivity to danger, but in a professional determination to ignore it in the interests of his job."[19]

The danger reporters faced was very real. On several occasions, Murrow was knocked down in the street by concussions from bomb blasts. Eric Sevareid told of the time that he, Murrow, and CBS colleague Larry LeSueur had just left the BBC building: "We heard nothing, but Murrow suddenly stepped into a doorway and Larry and I immediately followed suit. At that moment a jagged casing from an antiaircraft shell crashed precisely where we had been." Despite close calls, Murrow stayed out of shelters except to pursue a story. "Once you start going into shelters," he said, "you lose your nerve."[20] His listeners recognized Murrow's peril and his courage, which was like that of so many Londoners. It reminded the audience of the contrast between British bravery and American timidity in dealing with Germany.

Not all the correspondents stood up so well to the stress of a dangerous job. Sevareid later wrote that "a tin hat on your head made you feel far more secure, and it was good when you were with someone else in the exploding streets. If you were with a person less brave than yourself, you were braver than you would have been alone; if he were braver than you, you tried to emulate his behavior." Sevareid also wrote that he sometimes was unable to tolerate the shaking of the BBC building when a raid was underway, and so, "when there was no broadcast errand to be run, I found myself going down to the basement shelter, which seemed somehow ignoble."[21]

Murrow was steadier than that. Many nights he and Larry LeSueur would have dinner at L'Etoile restaurant on Charlotte Street, making sure to sit under a skylight, and then they would don their tin helmets—Murrow's had a noticeable shrapnel dent in it—and walk a few blocks to the BBC building.

Members of the CBS crew spent much of their time at the BBC, which monitored radio news from around the world and was kept informed by the government about home front developments. These were journalists together, sharing professional duties and, often, political sympathies. Murrow and his colleagues also gravitated to the BBC building because they were bombed out of their own offices several times and finally ended up putting what was left of their furniture and files in an apartment down the street from the Murrows' flat.

The British government understood the power and value of a steady flow of news, and treated the BBC as a part of the war effort. Entrances to the BBC building were manned by armed guards, and civilian BBC volunteers, some armed, patrolled within the building. The basement level concert hall had been stripped of its seats and turned into a dormitory (with blankets hanging across the middle of the room to separate the men's and women's areas). There was also an underground first-aid station, which received a bloody initiation in October when a bomb hit the building and killed seven people. In a sub-basement, a newsroom was set up, guarded by a machine gun nest in the balcony above it—part of the plan to defend this essential communications center for as long as possible in the event of an invasion. A small room well below street level was used by the Americans for their broadcasts.[22]

In 1940, about 150 American correspondents were working in Britain, most of whom were concentrated in the offices of the Associated Press, United Press, the *New York Times*, and the Hearst services. In dealing with the Americans, the BBC was careful not to seem to be playing favorites. To ensure that no one could claim that a competitor had received an exclusive, the BBC paired American correspondents for visits to airfields and training camps, ride-alongs in bombers and ambulances, and other officially sanctioned events. On their return to the BBC building, each would broadcast his own account. For these stories, Murrow was sometimes accompanied by NBC's Fred Bate, who later said of the attempt at evenhandedness, "The difference was that CBS had something we didn't have—Ed Murrow." Even though NBC's stories were close to those of CBS in number and general content, the rival network had no one who could match Murrow's on-air style or growing star power.[23]

Murrow began his reports with a signature phrase, "This is

London." It was suggested to him by Ida Lou Anderson, who had been his speech teacher at Washington State University and remained his mentor until her death in 1941. She urged him to avoid the trite, "Hello, America, this is London calling," which he had been considering, and instead use the shorter form. She also recommended that he accentuate "This" and understate "is London." There is no pause after "This," just a downshift into the next words.[24]

At the root of Murrow's journalistic success was good fundamental reporting. He had an eye for the bits and pieces that could be pulled together to form an expansive mosaic. Also, he worked constantly. In early December he told his listeners that after finishing broadcasts at around one in the morning, "there is no desire to sleep, only the urge to go out and walk familiar streets at a time when the night is left to darkness and to me." These walks could be exciting, he said, because "there may be fires, gunfire, and bombs" and one might see "human beings, looking like broken, cast-away, dust-covered barrels, being lifted with careful hands out of a tunnel driven through to the basement of a bombed house." At dawn, as the "all clear" signal sounded, "hundreds of thousands of humans come oozing up from underground, many of them stiff and tired from a night in the shelter. The ducks in Green Park set up their questioning quacking and the pigeons come back from some mysterious place to Trafalgar Square. Buckets of boiling water are poured into the muzzles of hard-worked guns, as they are swabbed out and prepared for another night's work."[25]

In addition to relying on sharp observation and crisp writing, Murrow and his colleagues continued to experiment with radio technique. According to Sevareid, they pulled together "the 'hard news' of the day, the feel of the scene, the quality of the big or little men involved, the meaning and implications of whatever had happened. All the rigid, traditional formulae of news writing had to be thrown out of the window, and a new kind of pertinent, contemporary essay became the standard form."[26] Murrow was always ready to be creative with the audio aspects of these essays, calling listeners' attention to sounds in the background and on one occasion setting his microphone on the sidewalk to capture the tap-tap-tap of Londoners' footsteps as they went determinedly about their business.

It was all done live. The BBC offered to make recording equipment available to CBS and others, but the U.S. networks turned them down. The reason was rooted in the economics of broadcasting. A network at that time was basically nothing more than leased lines that fed programming to affiliates, and if recordings were used, why would affiliates need a network? A later radio journalist, Bob Edwards of National Public Radio, explained that "the networks carried live broadcasts by the best orchestras. If a network played recordings of those orchestras, it would be doing nothing more than its affiliated stations could do for themselves. So the networks permitted no recordings, and the sounds of World War II could be heard only if a reporter happened to be broadcasting from the scene of conflict."[27]

Murrow was always looking for new vantage points. He sometimes went to Shakespeare Cliff, near Dover, where he could look up and see dogfights between Spitfires and Messerschmitts. Sevareid recalled that from the cliffs he and Murrow "looked across at the narrow film on the water which was the coast of France, where the enemy was looking across at us. We watched the planes come over, tiny white feathers most of the time against the stratosphere. We grabbed our hats as the concussion of defense guns flapped our clothes and yelled in excitement at the brief, bright speckle in the blue, like a match lighted a mile away, which meant one plane down in flames."[28]

As in the coverage of any war, there was plenty of tension between journalists who were digging for stories and government bureaucrats who tried to control the digging. Murrow and his colleagues wanted news; the government wanted its story presented to the public in the best possible light. Those goals were often incompatible. Just a few days before the blitz began, a meeting was held at the Ministry of Information to discuss American reporters' request to be allowed to cover air raids in progress.

Military and civilian officials had many objections: the enemy would gain useful information from such reports; morale would sink; the public would become angry if its suffering was highlighted. The more perceptive MoI representatives argued the other side—that what mattered most was that these broadcasts would be useful "in persuading America to give more help to this country." The meeting ended without a policy being settled upon, but two weeks after the blitz began, Murrow was given the go-ahead to do his reports while attacks on London were underway.[29]

Murrow barraged the BBC liaison office with proposals for stories that he wanted to do. During the summer of 1940, he asked to send reporters in many directions: to Gibraltar, to Cairo, on a naval vessel in the Bristol Channel, on torpedo boat patrol, to an observation post on the coast, on a patrol flight from Scotland to Norway, to an internment camp, to the London docks where food and other necessities were being unloaded, to the Bow Street police court to show British justice being applied to minor offenses. . . . While one list was being considered, Murrow was working on the next one. The BBC's Roger Eckersley did his best; for this particular list he got approval for the observation post, the docks, and the court, a definite rejection for Gibraltar, and a lingering maybe for the others.[30]

Eckersley was a forceful advocate, making Murrow's case to the Ministry of Information gatekeepers. He told the MoI's Frank Darvall that Murrow and NBC's Fred Bate could be trusted not to sensationalize their coverage of air raids in progress—"they are not the sort of people who would pile on horror, but at the same time they would expect to be allowed to be factual in a quiet way."[31]

Murrow kept the pressure on, sometimes with sharp jabs to underscore his point. In October 1940, for instance, he asked to be allowed to send CBS correspondent Larry LeSueur to Iceland and told Eckersley, "I do think that a couple of talks from the one area successfully invaded by Britain would have a salubrious effect on our audience." The trip was approved.[32]

Censorship continued to obstruct reporting and Murrow

addressed it on the air in November 1940 after a meeting with the minister of information, Alfred Duff Cooper. "After more than a year of practice," said Murrow, "the system remains unpredictable and erratic. It is still the most liberal system of censorship in Europe, but sometimes, in an effort to mislead Britain's enemies, it succeeds only in misleading or confusing her friends." Duff Cooper stood his ground, but, said Murrow, "the American correspondents left him in no doubt as to the objection to his censorship department."[33] The stalemate persisted, alleviated somewhat by the arrival in the MoI ranks of more officials with journalistic experience. Murrow also noted that despite restrictions his American listeners were receiving more information about the war than were members of the British public.

Some journalists just dealt with the censorship rather than fighting it. American newspaperman Ernie Pyle, who reported from London for several months in early 1941, found it to be only a minor problem. "There are only a few general subjects that you're forbidden to mention," he wrote, "such as troop movements, the location of guns, and the location of any specific bombings until after a certain amount of time has elapsed. There are also other items, such as not giving out current weather conditions or the routes of ships or planes or cabling anything about a fire until it is out. The best thing about the press censorship here is that you always know what is being cut out. The censor calls you on the telephone. And you can even argue with him. Of course you usually lose out, but imagine arguing with the censor in some countries!" He added that the British authorities "don't censor opinion. If you wanted to, you could say that you think England stinks, and it would go through. I think the censorship has allowed America to get a pretty honest picture of what has happened over here."[34]

The censors' watchfulness did not stop tales of life during the blitz from proliferating both in England and abroad. Besides the stories about destruction and heroism, light anecdotes abounded, with the line between the true and the apocryphal often blurry. When the Carlton Club, a Conservative Party bastion in London, was badly damaged by bombs and Churchill remarked that he was surprised that no one had been killed, a Labor Party official replied, "The devil looks after his own." A sign on a church door told frightened parishioners, "If your knees knock, kneel on them." During a raid, a nanny reminded her young charge, "Yes, that was probably bombs, Master James, but that's no excuse for elbows on the table." A sign on a bombed shop said: "Hitler was our last customer. Will you be the next? We're still open."[35] Vignettes of "those plucky Brits" were nurtured by the British government as yet another tool to maintain morale at home and win admirers in America.

But British historian Philip Ziegler has written that such stories and some of the tales of bravery were part of a "myth of the blitz" that Londoners created in an effort to show the world that they remained nonchalant in the face of danger. American journalists such as Murrow, wrote Ziegler, "contributed as much as anyone to the propagation of the myth. . . . They tended to be less critical in their assessment of London under fire than any British commentator would have dared to be. Anything that contributed to the vision of a society of stout-hearted, yet self-deprecating heroes was written up, anything that savored of greed, cowardice, any sort of baseness, was rigorously eschewed. It was a propaganda exercise conducted with great skill, and one for which the British had cause to be grateful."[36]

For example, several weeks into the blitz Murrow told his listeners that "to me one of the most impressive things about talking with Londoners these days is this—there's no mention of money," and although people might describe the damage done to their homes they would not talk about the monetary value of what was lost or how much the rebuilding would cost.[37] Of course, for many Londoners money was very much an issue as they contemplated their uncertain future, and there was a dark side to their concerns as well: price-gouging, a thriving black market, and other problems that the government addressed with mixed success. All was not hope and glory, despite the depictions of Britain that most Americans became familiar with.

❋   ❋   ❋   ❋

Murrow's portrayals of England at war were buttressed by other versions delivered to America by other messengers. Ernie Pyle came to Britain at the end of 1940 to cover the blitz for the Scripps-Howard newspaper chain. He had planned to stay for one month but remained for three. He quickly determined that the spirit of London had not been gravely injured, reporting in December that so far, "the blitz on London is a failure." Nevertheless, he was awed when he saw London "ringed and stabbed by fire." A few days after Christmas, he wrote about "the monstrous loveliness of that one single view of London on a holiday night—London stabbed with great fires, shaken by explosions, its dark regions along the Thames sparkling with the pinpoints of white-hot bombs, all of it roofed over with a ceiling of pink that held bursting shells, balloons, flares, and the grind of vicious engines. And in yourself, the excitement and anticipation and wonder in your soul that this could be happening at all. These things all went together to make the most hateful, most beautiful single scene I have ever known."[38]

Pyle immersed himself in the life of London, captivated by the daily sights and sounds of the wartime city. Of the air raid sirens, he wrote: "To me, the sirens do not sound fiendish, or even weird. I think they're sort of pretty. The other night when the all-clear sounded I lay on the bed listening. You could hear half a dozen sirens going at once, on exactly the same pitch. The combined whirring of these great horns out there in the still darkness gave off a sort of musical pulsation. In fact, it sounded exactly like the lonely singing of telephone wires on a bitter cold night in the prairies of the Middle West."[39]

Some of Pyle's reporting had a light touch, as when he described how one hotel had set aside a separate area in its shelter for chronic snorers: "They just herd 'em all together and let 'em snore it out." But he never lost sight of the reality of life under siege. Just before he returned to America in March 1941, he wrote:

"There is a lot of sudden dying in London every night. It is hit-and-skip dying. It is death dealt by mystic lottery. A lone bomber three miles above in the dark lets one loose." Despite the constant presence of death from the skies, wrote Pyle, "In three months I have not met an Englishman to whom it has ever occurred that Britain might lose the war."[40]

Also reporting from London was *The New Yorker's* Mollie Painter-Downes, who, like her colleagues, examined how one lived under the constant menace of German air raids. "For Londoners," she wrote, "there are no longer such things as good nights; there are only bad nights, worse nights, and better nights. . . . The blitzkrieg continues to be directed against such military objectives as the tired shopgirl, the red-eyed clerk, and the thousands of dazed and weary families patiently trundling their few belongings in perambulators away from the wreckage of their homes."[41] As with Murrow's reporting, Painter-Downes's work helped Americans identify with the "people like us" in her pieces.

Yet another way Americans received news of Britain was through BBC essayists such as J. B. Priestley. A veteran of World War I, Priestley was a popular novelist and playwright whose radio talks in 1940 featured working-class Britons as heroes and extolled England's willingness to fight on, whatever the odds. Describing the angered Englishman, he said: "You know how it is with a bulldog. He'll let you tease him and maul him for perhaps an hour or two, but go an inch too far and he'll sink his teeth into you and never let go. Well, that's the real English, the ordinary quiet folk."[42]

Like other commentators, Priestley described the fire-ravaged city, as in this broadcast during the beginning of the blitz: "From where I watched, the greatest of the fires was just behind St. Paul's, which was carefully silhouetted in dead black against the red glare of the flames and the orange-pink of the smoke. It stood there like a symbol—with its unbroken dome and towering cross—of an enduring civilization of reason and Christian ethics against a red menacing glare of unreason, destruction, and savagery."[43]

Beyond such observations, Priestley's approach—encouraged by the Ministry of Information—was not to explicitly call for American belligerency, but rather to make Americans feel ashamed that they were not doing enough to aid gallant Britain. "Though my American friends feel all the horror and anguish of this time just as we do," he said, "they are really worse off in mind and spirit now than we are, because they can only stare at the dreadful scene in terror and pity, like people on the seashore who watch a great ship struggling against a terrible storm. But we, who are on the ship and in the storm, are now so completely engrossed in action that there comes to us, as a compensation for all our effort, a certain feeling of expansion, a heightening of the spirit, a sense that somewhere in this struggle of free men against drilled and doped slaves there is a moral grandeur. Soon, some of us may die, but nobody can say of us now that we are not alive. . . . So I say, do not pity us."[44]

Priestley could bristle as well. When an American listener wrote to argue that America should remain behind "her own impregnable ramparts," Priestley said in a broadcast: "The fact is, you haven't impregnable ramparts. The only impregnable ramparts that the Nazis would recognize are vast navies, air forces, and armies, and at the moment you haven't got them." The same letter writer, who was from Glens Falls, New York, accused England of fighting only to preserve its empire. Priestley responded: "Great Britain is fighting to rescue Europe today, and the rest of the world tomorrow, from the domination of a gang of liars, looters, and murderers, who wherever they have gone so far have destroyed human liberty and all possibility of real progress. If Glens Falls does not recognize these facts, then Glens Falls is both blind and deaf."[45]

During the first days of the blitz, Priestley told America that Britain would prevail against Hermann Goering's Luftwaffe: "The islanders set their jaws and defy his bombers, which fall through the air like rotten fruit; and the terrible game of total war, which these evil men planned and once rejoiced in, will be played to a finish. . . . So long as our people feel they can hit back—and we're going to hit back harder and harder—Goering will never bomb them into suing for terms even if he sends over, night after night, every machine he's got. . . . You carry on, happily conscious of the fact that you are in the midst of a great battle and appear to be winning it. And I'll bet that's more than Goering can say."[46]

While the BBC delivered Priestley into American homes, Murrow was using media other than radio to expand his reporting about how Britain was faring. He wrote the preface to a book of photographs of beleaguered Britain that was published in England as *Grim Glory* and in America as *Bloody but Unbowed*. "These are pictures of a nation at war," he wrote. "They are honest pictures—routine scenes to those of us who have reported Britain's ordeal by fire and high explosive. These Englishmen have bought survival with their tender-roofed old buildings, with their bodies and their nerves. This little book offers you a glimpse of their battle. Somehow they are able to fight down their fears each night, to go to work each morning. . . . Much history has been blasted apart in Britain; but only the symbols are gone."[47]

Murrow continued his appearances on BBC programs, presenting talks about American politics and the impressions of "An American Journalist in London Now."[48] He also narrated a British-made documentary, *This Is England*, which was widely screened in the United States, thanks in part to being touted by FDR aide Harry Hopkins, and was well received by American audiences. The narration—over pictures of charred Coventry Cathedral and waves of British bombers headed for Germany—promised that "the Nazis will learn once and for all that no one with impunity troubles the heart of Britain."[49]

As in many of his radio broadcasts, in these other ventures Murrow focused on the average Briton. In *Bloody but Unbowed* he wrote that "the spirit of men who made Britain great still walks the streets in the shape of little men who think of themselves only as Englishmen." The defiant Churchill persona was well established by this time, as was the heroism of the RAF pilots who were fighting the Battle of Britain, but Murrow wanted to establish empathy at a more personal level between the average

American and the average, "little" Englishman. Conveying that sense of kinship, more than describing high-level politics, was likely to nudge Americans closer to feeling that they had friends in Britain whom they should help. This was propaganda as much as it was news, but the line between the two could become indistinct in some of Murrow's work.

These Murrow projects were part of the ongoing effort by the British government to use mass media to make its case to Americans. Murrow's work was bolstered by other Americans. Quentin Reynolds narrated the film *Britain Can Take It,* which was produced by the Ministry of Information. As always, the British did not want to appear too overt in their propaganda efforts, so when the film was shown in the United States, it was distributed by Warner Brothers and the MoI was not mentioned in the credits. It was a great popular success; it opened in November 1940 and by the following spring it had been shown in 12,000 movie theaters and seen by an estimated sixty million Americans.[50] It was one more version of heroic Britain. Over scenes of devastation from the bombing and portraits of courageous air raid wardens and others, Reynolds said: "It is true that the Nazis will be over again tomorrow night and the night after that and every night. They will drop thousands of bombs and they'll destroy hundreds of buildings and they'll kill thousands of people. But a bomb has its limitations. It can only destroy buildings and kill people. It cannot kill the unconquerable spirit and courage of the people of Britain."[51]

Inspiring motion pictures were valuable, but day in and day out radio remained the most consistently effective venue for influencing opinion. By this point in the war, there was no need for subtlety when the British laid claim to moral superiority. On a BBC broadcast directed at Americans, Reverend Pat McCormick told listeners, "Britain and all that Britain stands for can never die; she is bound to win the day in the end, because she stands for the right, the good, the true, and the noble." Perhaps concerned that Reverend McCormick did not have enough audience appeal, the BBC teased Americans with this promotional message: "Don't forget Princess Elizabeth at 7:45 PM, Eastern Standard Time, next Sunday!" For various reasons, British radio programming developed a following among Americans, and U.S. broadcasting companies took note. By late 1940, eighty-eight American stations were relaying BBC news and the Mutual Broadcasting System was providing rebroadcasts of BBC news and talks.[52]

Meanwhile, American journalists in England were courted at the highest levels. When pro-intervention radio broadcaster Raymond Gram Swing visited London, Churchill invited him to a small luncheon at which Harry Hopkins was also a guest. The prime minister then had a long private conversation with Swing.[53] Churchill talked with Americans such as Hopkins and Swing not only to make Britain's case but also to ask questions and gain insight into U.S. politics and policy. At Downing Street and at the Foreign Office, the work of American journalists was scrutinized with increasing care as Churchill's government tried to anticipate movement in American attitudes and shifts in U.S. policy. Ronald Tree said of the United States, "There is no country in the world where public opinion is more volatile or changes quicker, and at the same time in which public opinion plays a more decisive role in molding policy."[54]

An article by Swing that was published in London's *Sunday Express* in early 1941 explained Roosevelt's strategy of not wanting to "appear to be 'taking' the country into war" for fear that public opinion would turn against him. Rather, the president wanted to wait for opinion to shift so he could then "appear to have yielded to public insistence, and that war should be an enterprise of partnership rather than something entered at his behest." Swing urged Americans to be more impatient, but added that "in Britain patience must rise in the same degree." British policymakers may not have liked the state of affairs reflected by Swing's message, but a number of top Foreign Office officials acknowledged that his appraisal was correct.[55]

Countering the pro-British slant of Murrow and other London-based reporters, isolationist voices in the news media made themselves heard, even during the blitz. On the Mutual network in late September 1940, Fulton Lewis, Jr., contradicted the reports from Murrow and others about "the real situation" in England. He was particularly critical of the photographs from London that had been appearing in American newspapers: "Now you've doubtless seen pictures of these various sites, buildings, ruins, and blazing fires because those are the only things photographers take pictures of. There's no news interest in taking pictures of the buildings that are not injured." He added that the German raids were "not nearly as efficient as they have been advertised."[56] As it happened, the night after Lewis's broadcast Murrow reported from a London rooftop "watching as the bombers came in." He did not apparently notice any inefficiency on the Germans' part.

❋　❋　❋　❋

The impact of Murrow's reporting and Churchill's cajoling was limited because of Roosevelt's increasing caution as the presidential election drew nearer. FDR's handling of Joseph Kennedy illustrated how carefully he intended to proceed. In October 1940, after serving two years and nine months as ambassador, Kennedy returned to America. The final months of his tenure had been difficult in part because neither Roosevelt nor Churchill fully trusted him. The president worried that Kennedy's defeatist pronouncements could damage his reelection campaign, and the prime minister never forgave Kennedy for his infatuation with the appeasement clique.

Kennedy's letters during the blitz reflected compassion for Britons' suffering, but he never understood how determination and anger could keep England afloat amidst the physical destruction the Germans were inflicting. He privately told friends that he thought Britain would fold once its financial resources ran out, and his official analyses were similarly downbeat. In a cable to the State Department shortly before his departure, he wrote, "I cannot impress upon you strongly enough my complete lack of confidence in the entire conduct of this war."[57]

Despite the tension between Kennedy and the Churchill

government, the British press treated him gently when he departed. Kennedy responded generously, saying: "I did not know London could take it. I did not think any city could take it. I am bowed in reverence."[58]

Kennedy arrived in New York less than two weeks before the election, and Republicans hoped that he might endorse Wendell Willkie and denounce Roosevelt for conniving to take America into the European war. But before Kennedy could be captured by the Republicans he was summoned to the White House, where the president listened sympathetically as he rolled through his litany of complaints about how badly he had been treated by the State Department. FDR promised "a real housecleaning" of State Department bureaucrats and then asked Kennedy to give a radio speech endorsing his reelection. Kennedy's anger was no match for Roosevelt's charm, particularly when Roosevelt—according to John F. Kennedy years later—hinted that he would like to see Joe Kennedy as the 1944 Democratic presidential nominee. Another incentive—according to Joseph Kennedy himself, also years later—was a promise by FDR to support Joseph Kennedy, Jr., for governor of Massachusetts in 1942.[59] (Joe, Jr., was later killed in the war.)

Although Kennedy tried to create suspense in the press about whom he would endorse, he had decided, for whatever reason, to stand with Roosevelt. In his nationally broadcast radio speech, Kennedy said: "Unfortunately during this political campaign, there has arisen the charge that the president of the United States is trying to involve this country in a world war. Such a charge is false." He said that although he may have occasionally disagreed with Roosevelt's positions on some issues, the time was not right for a new president to take charge. "The man of experience," said Kennedy "is our man of the hour."[60]

The speech was judged a great success and the Republicans were deprived of a last-minute boost. Roosevelt and Kennedy appeared together at a campaign rally in Boston at which the president, addressing himself to the "mothers and fathers of America," promised, "Your boys are not going to be sent into any foreign wars." This same pledge had been incorporated in the Democratic Party platform earlier that year, except the platform added the condition, "except in case of attack." When Roosevelt left that phrase out of his Boston speech, one of his aides asked him why, and the president replied with fine Rooseveltian logic: "Of course we'll fight if we're attacked. If somebody attacks us, then it isn't a foreign war, is it?"[61]

After Roosevelt defeated Willkie, Kennedy hoped to be rewarded for his loyalty, perhaps with a cabinet post. Discreet silence about Britain would have served him well, but instead he talked himself into trouble. He told Assistant Secretary of State Breckinridge Long that the United States should adopt a "realistic policy" that included economic collaboration with Germany and Japan. Several days later, Kennedy gave a long interview to the *Boston Globe* in which he said: "Democracy is finished in England. It may be here. Because it comes to a question of feeding people. It's all an economic question." This reflected Kennedy's view that war was likely to require increased government control to the point of fascism, but news accounts of the interview did not address economic theory. Kennedy's first sentence was the headline for newspaper stories around the world. He dug a deeper hole for himself by making more defeatist comments to acquaintances in California, including FDR's son-in-law John Boettiger.[62]

Finally, Roosevelt summoned Kennedy to a face-to-face meeting at Hyde Park. Now that the election was past, Roosevelt had no need to propitiate the former ambassador, and Kennedy's repeated insistence that Britain was no match for the unbeatable German military so infuriated the president that he summoned Eleanor and told her to take Kennedy with her, give him lunch at her cottage, and put him on the train.[63]

Across the Atlantic, patience with Kennedy had also been exhausted. Churchill sarcastically referred to Kennedy's comments about the death of democracy as a parting salute to the island race. In the *Daily Mail*, an open letter to Kennedy said: "How little you know us, after all. Your three years as ambassador have given you no insight into the character and traditions of the British people."[64]

The attention paid in Britain to the Kennedy controversy was one facet of the continuing fixation on America's political mood. Mollie Painter-Downes wrote: "The press and the public here devote considerable space and time to what America is saying, doing and thinking. As men once watched the East for a portent, millions are now looking to the West with hope and confidence." Murrow reported a shift in British officials' outlook: "Some would express a preference for winning the war without American aid, but most would admit that it can't be done. I'm reporting what I believe to be the dominant informed opinion in this country, [which is] British belief that a democratic nation at peace cannot render full and effective support to a nation at war." In other words, aid from a non-belligerent would not be enough; America had to wade into the fight. Murrow added one of his disclaimers that as usual underscored the opinion that he said he was suppressing: "As a reporter I'm concerned to report this development, not to evaluate it in terms of personal approval or disapproval."[65]

In America, debate became even more intense. In his book *Against This Torrent*, Princeton University professor Edward Mead Earle argued against Kennedy-style defeatism and the nonchalant caution of many others. He wrote: "It is incredible that there should be a single American to say that the outcome of this struggle is a matter of indifference to the United States. On the contrary, with the possible exception of Secession, we have never before faced a crisis of such moment to our future." If Britain were to be defeated, he added, "we shall become a besieged fortress, a garrison state. And even then we shall have no assurance of security from attack. This truly appalling prospect would mean an end to American institutions and the American standard of living as we have known them. Only by effective resistance now can we avoid so grave a tragedy to all that we hold dear."[66]

That was one example of how members of America's academic and journalistic intelligentsia were becoming more overtly supportive of Britain. In a January 1941 letter to British diplomat

Harold Nicolson, journalist Walter Lippmann wrote that "the intellectual conviction is general that American security is directly involved with the British cause. But it is the courage of the British people which has won the hearts of the people here. The effect has been immense—no one dares to be openly anti-British and the overwhelming majority are for the first time in my lifetime really pro-British." Lippmann said that the slowness to act was caused primarily by "the fear of being engaged in war before we are fully armed. . . . In proportion as you convince the American people of your determination and capacity to hold out and as our own armament program begins to produce real results, which it will in a reasonably short time now, the willingness to take action here will grow greater." In a letter to another British friend, Sibyl Colefax, Lippmann noted that Americans were watching carefully how the British were bearing up under the German siege. He wrote that "American optimism and pessimism and our morale is, and will continue to be, a reflection of yours. . . . What the British people and spokesmen say and feel is critical for what we feel and say."[67]

Lippmann's attention to "the courage of the British people" and to the pronouncements of "the British people and spokesmen" makes clear the importance of the depictions of Britain provided by Murrow and others. Americans were "watching carefully," as Lippmann said, and journalists on the scene served as their eyes.

Despite the perception that U.S. support for Britain was becoming firmer, American news organizations remained cautious about appearing to tilt toward intervention. In early 1941, Vincent Sheean traveled on a British destroyer engaged in the dangerous work of protecting a convoy. At the end of his *Saturday Evening Post* article about the voyage he wrote, "When our hour strikes, I hope our own navy will do as well." The magazine's editors removed that sentence.[68]

Roosevelt, meanwhile, was strengthening his political position before he provided more significant help to Britain. Prior to the 1940 election, he brought two prominent Republicans into his cabinet: as secretary of war, Henry L. Stimson, who had held the same job under President William Howard Taft and had been Herbert Hoover's secretary of state; and, as secretary of the Navy, Frank Knox, the publisher of the *Chicago Daily News*, who had been the Republican vice presidential nominee in 1936.

Then, less than two months after his election victory, FDR delivered one of the most important speeches of his presidency. He said at the outset that "the Nazi masters of Germany have made it clear that they intend not only to dominate all life and thought in their own country, but also to enslave the whole of Europe, and then to use the resources of Europe to dominate the rest of the world." He argued that "frankly and definitely there is danger ahead—danger against which we must prepare. But we well know that we cannot escape danger, or the fear of it, by crawling into bed and pulling the covers over our heads. . . . The experience of the past two years has proven beyond doubt that no nation can appease the Nazis. No man can tame a tiger into a kitten by stroking it." He tied America's future to the outcome of Britain's struggle and said, "I make the direct statement to the American people that there is far less chance of the United States getting into war if we do all we can now to support the nations defending themselves against attack by the Axis than if we acquiesce in their defeat, submit tamely to an Axis victory, and wait our turn to be the object of attack in another war later on." As for America's immediate role, Roosevelt said: "We must be the great arsenal of democracy. For this is an emergency as serious as war itself. We must apply ourselves to our task with the same resolution, the same sense of urgency, the same spirit of patriotism and sacrifice as we would show were we at war."

Roosevelt followed this declaration of almost-war with the unveiling of his Lend-Lease plan, which would allow him to deliver war material to Britain even when she could no longer pay for it. His timing was perfect; public opinion in support of helping Britain had reached the level at which he could build his aid measures on relatively firm political ground. Polling found that 61 percent of those who heard the "arsenal of democracy" speech agreed with it, and the White House reported that mail and telegrams ran a hundred to one in favor of the president's position.[69] At the same time, the Gallup Poll was finding a significant shift in responses to the question, "Do you think the United States should keep out of war or do everything possible to help England even at the risk of getting into war ourselves?" In May 1940, the answers ran 64 percent "stay out" to 36 percent "risk war"; in November, the answers were 50-50; in December, 40 percent said "stay out" while 60 percent said "help England."[70] The popular support that allowed Roosevelt to move ahead came just in time for Churchill, who especially needed the destroyers that were part of the American aid program. British shipping was being ravaged by the Germans: 365,000 tons a month were lost during the winter of 1940–41; by April the figure was up to 687,000 tons a month.[71] If allowed to continue, losses of this magnitude would strangle Britain.

Just as the merchant shipping fleet was depleted, so too were the British financial reserves nearly exhausted. Cash-and-carry purchasing of needed war material could not continue indefinitely. Roosevelt took advantage of an 1892 statute that allowed the secretary of war to lease military property for up to five years, and the president devised a way of doing so that put little further burden on the British. In a mid-December press conference, Roosevelt explained his rationale: "Suppose my neighbor's home catches on fire, and I have a length of garden hose four or five hundred feet away. If he can take my garden hose and connect it up with his hydrant, I may help to put out his fire. Now what do I do? I don't say to him, 'Neighbor, my garden hose cost me fifteen dollars, so you must give me fifteen dollars.' . . . I don't want fifteen dollars—I want my garden hose back after the fire is over. If the hose is damaged, my neighbor can repair or replace it."[72]

Churchill wrote that "there was no provision for repayment. There was not even to be a formal account kept in dollars or sterling. What we had was lent or leased to us because our continued resistance to the Hitler tyranny was deemed to be of vital interest to the great Republic."[73] Roosevelt was more succinct.

When he was asked by reporters who would hold legal title to the military equipment, he said, "I don't know and I don't care."[74]

In a private letter to King George, Roosevelt wrote, "In regard to materials from here, I am, as you know, doing everything possible in the way of acceleration and in the way of additional release of literally everything that we can spare." Noting that he appreciated "how splendidly all of your good people are standing up under these terrific air attacks," Roosevelt said, "All that is being done in Great Britain and the way it is being done make me feel very futile with respect to our own efforts." He added that the "destroyer arrangement seems to have worked out perfectly. There is virtually no criticism in this country except from legalists who think it should have been submitted to the Congress first. If I had done that, the subject would still be in the tender care of the committees of the Congress!"[75]

Churchill later described Roosevelt's initiative as "the most unsordid act in the history of any nation." In a radio address in February 1941, Churchill spoke to Roosevelt and the American people: "Put your confidence in us. Give us your faith and your blessing, and, under Providence, all will be well. We shall not fail or falter; we shall not weaken or tire. Neither the sudden shock of battle nor the long-drawn trials of vigilance and exertion will wear us down. Give us the tools and we will finish the job."[76]

✻   ✻   ✻   ✻

As was the case with most Londoners, the lives of Ed and Janet Murrow were being reshaped by the blitz. Ed booked passage for Janet to return to America, but she wouldn't go. She believed a wife should stay with her husband and said, "It won't be worse for me than anybody else."[77] She had gotten a terrifying early sense of what it was like to be bombed. On the first day of the blitz, she went up to the roof of their apartment building at 84 Hallam Street to take a look. As the sound of the planes grew louder and shrapnel began spattering around her, she found that the door to the roof had locked behind her. She shouted and waved to pedestrians on the street below, but they were intent on finding shelter and no one heard or saw her. Finally someone spotted her and ran up six flights of stairs to open the door.[78]

She spent many nights of intense bombing alone, waiting for Ed. In one of her letters home she wrote: "Last night was one of the worst nights we've had. I had put little mattresses out in the hall for the purpose of sleeping if the occasion arose. At about midnight last night I decided that the hour had come. So I took my pillows and a blanket out into the corridor and curled up and slept rather well considering the fact that bombs dropped rather close and there were several fires round about. About 4:30 in the morning Ed almost walked over me."[79]

On this night as on so many others, Ed had been out roaming through the city after his broadcast. He would sometimes not return from watching the fires until dawn, and he subsisted largely on coffee and cigarettes, losing thirty pounds during the blitz. Janet had given up smoking, so Ed got her American Embassy cigarette ration and smoked up to eighty cigarettes a day. The stress on both of them was constant, produced not just by the physical dangers of the bombing but also by the exhaustion and tension that accompanied Ed's work. There were missed meals and cancelled evenings out, and Janet sometimes felt that she had been set aside to exist on her own outside Ed's life. Ed seemed to recognize, at least occasionally, how difficult things were for her. In a letter to his parents he acknowledged that Janet "did not have much of a life," and, he said, "she doesn't complain, although I can't see why she doesn't. . . . She is the world's best and I love her deeply." Writing to Janet's parents about his reporting, he said: "Janet is responsible for whatever balance and honesty there has been in it. We are happy even in the midst of all this."[80]

Janet structured her life around Ed's schedule and needs. When Ed returned to the apartment in the early morning hours, she often had sandwiches and coffee waiting, even if she had already gone to bed. Ed sometimes brought people home with him—BBC colleagues and friends such as Czech foreign minister Jan Masaryk—regardless of the time. They would talk for hours on end, sometimes over poker games in which Ed was known for his daring betting. One colleague wrote that Murrow frequently lost "because the courage of his convictions did not match his cards."[81]

Even these diversions were colored by the reality that fell from the skies every night and the fears that, even if controlled, were inescapable. Janet wrote to their parents about Ed's job: "The work is dangerous, terribly dangerous, compared to life at home, but no more dangerous here for one person than another. Ed doesn't take unnecessary chances, I think, so don't worry about him more than you can help."[82] Despite the calming words, Ed and Janet both had close calls. One night, as they walked home from dinner, Ed wanted to stop for a drink at a neighborhood pub, but Janet heard planes in the distance and insisted that they go straight to the apartment. Moments later, they had to run for cover as they heard the *whoosh* of a bomb dropping toward them. It narrowly missed their building, and the pub that they had just walked away from had been blown apart. The neighborhood was on fire and the CBS office down the street had been hit. Ed rushed there to find that his secretary, Kay Campbell, had been thrown by the blast through an open doorway but was not badly hurt. (By spring 1941, the CBS team was in its fourth office after having been bombed out of the previous three.) On another night, the Murrows were in their apartment talking with a visitor from America and Ed was describing the sound of incendiary bombs hitting: "Swish-swash, and then a plunk." There seemed to be an echo: "Swish-swash . . . plunk." They ran upstairs and found that incendiaries had hit their roof. They were in time to smother them with shovelfuls of sand.[83]

There was occasional respite. Ronald and Nancy Tree invited Janet and Ed to Ditchley and Lady Milner urged them to come on a weekend to Great Wigsell. Janet enjoyed her lofty social contacts but knew better than to take them or herself too seriously. She wrote to her brother: "I was presented to the Queen on Tuesday and on Wednesday had lunch sitting on the Prime Minister's right hand. I'm pretty impressed with myself."[84]

Janet threw herself into her work with "Bundles for Britain," which she enjoyed and believed was making a substantive contribution to the British war effort. She remained well aware of the realities of London under attack. For example, she knew that the underground shelters, depicted so often as places of cheerful camaraderie, were in truth foul refuges. "Sanitation and ventilation are terrible," she wrote. "The stench coming from the entrance to a subway is enough to sicken anyone. How people manage to sleep there is beyond me."[85]

She was moved by the plight of Londoners and later described the rest centers established for blitz victims: "The bombed-out people arrive clutching a dog, a canary, a pillow . . . anything they have been able to grab when the bomb fell. First, they're given a hot drink; then, given some warm clothing, wrapped in a blanket, put to bed on a mattress on the floor, and—believe it or not—they generally sleep, although the night is still noisy and the bombs are still falling. By the time morning comes the order has gone through to the central regional depot for a further supply of clothing to more adequately fit out the homeless people. It's so important to get them back to work at the usual hours so that not a moment will be lost in making the weapons of war."[86]

Although she enjoyed a far better life than did most Londoners, Janet was being worn down by the blitz. "Before September," she wrote, "I had quite a few friends left in town. But I just don't know where they are now. You don't have time to see people for pleasure unless you can combine it with business. It takes ages to get a telephone call through and you don't bother. . . . In London, people work and go to their blacked-out hideaways and listen to bombs hurtling down and guns roaring and hope for the best. It's not a pleasant life and no one likes it. But everyone seems grateful to be alive."[87]

Seeking occasional respite from their schedule and the dangers they faced, she and Ed found a house to rent at 2 Maple Avenue in Bishops Stortford, which is on the road from London to Cambridge. Janet described "a nice big house and well furnished; four double bedrooms and drawing room, dining room, smoking room, and kitchen." She noted that it "is quite secluded, has a big garden and a nice lawn. It's an old-fashioned Victorian type of red brick." This was the unofficial CBS getaway spot. Ed tried to come twice a week for some bomb-free sleep and other CBS staff members came when they could. There were also weekend guests from their circle in London, such as the prime minister of the Netherlands.

Many others, driven from London by the bombing, also came to Bishops Stortford, and the town of 10,000 did its best to deal with the influx. Janet wrote that it was one of the first places to set up communal feeding of evacuees: "Everybody helps by giving some of the produce from their gardens."[88]

Having a place away from London meant a lot, particularly to Janet, because it provided snatches of time with less than usual stress. No one—not even the pluckiest Brit—could relax with bombs dropping. When the Bishops Stortford house was no longer available, she found another, in Bampton, near Oxford, that they would share with Ministry of Information official Frank Darvall and his wife Dorothy. Janet told her brother that it had a "large kitchen garden and lots of fruit. . . . a formal boxwood garden and a huge tennis lawn."[89]

Most Londoners had no idyllic retreats to escape to, but the Murrows did not try to prove a point or demonstrate how tough they were by barricading themselves in their Hallam Street flat. They were in the war but not part of it, at least not in the same way the British were, despite Ed's strong feelings about the need for America to assert itself. In his private expressions of opinion and in his broadcasts, he was becoming even more hawkish.

He had been watching people die and seeing a democratic nation throttled while his own country remained largely disengaged. While Janet was away from London one night he wrote her a note about what he was doing during those late nights at the broadcast center: "Have been doing some fair talking last few nights. Pulled out all the stops and let them have it. Now I think is the time. A thousand years of history and civilization are being smashed. Maybe the stuff I am doing is falling flat; would be better if you could look at it, but have spent three years trying to make people believe me and am now using that for all tis worth." His determination was mixed with frustration, which he displayed in a letter to a friend: "I know in my own mind that I have more and better information than ever before. But it's exceedingly difficult to know just what to do with it. I have no desire to use the studio as a privileged pulpit, but am convinced that some very plain talking is required in the immediate future, even if it be at the price of being labeled a warmonger." In another letter: "The thing that's most obvious is that if the light of the world is to come from the West, somebody had better start building some bonfires."[90]

He wrote to his parents to say that he had no plans to leave Britain: "This is the end of an age, the end of things I was taught to love and respect, and I must stay here and report it if it kills me. One life more or less means nothing. . . . Some people, many of whom I don't know, trust me and they can't be let down."[91]

While he was venting his frustrations in some of his correspondence, he was also helping British officials who traveled to America as part of the effort to influence U.S. policy. Murrow wrote to Justice Felix Frankfurter and others to urge them to talk with visiting British friends such as Ministry of Information officials Frank Darvall and Lindsay Wellington and *The Economist's* editor Geoffrey Crowther.

Murrow met several times in London with FDR's principal emissary, Harry Hopkins. Their first conversation was in January 1941, when Murrow went to Hopkins's room at Claridge's hotel for what he thought would be a conventional interview. Instead it turned out that Hopkins was intent on interviewing Murrow, questioning him at length about British politics and public morale. When Murrow asked him what he hoped to accomplish during his visit, Hopkins said, "I suppose you could say that I've come here to try to find a way to be a catalytic agent between two prima donnas." Anticipating a clash between the oversized egos of Roosevelt and Churchill, Hopkins wanted to learn as much as he could about the British leader—how he worked, whom he listened to—so he could be an effective mediator if the relationship ever became rocky. He said, "I want to try to get an understanding of Churchill and of the men he sees after midnight."[92]

Hopkins was well aware of Murrow's credibility with American audiences, and he urged him to come to the United States to "talk with a few people" on a speaking tour, the purpose of which would be to bolster Roosevelt's plans for Lend-Lease and further aid to Britain. Murrow declined and later told his brother Lacey, "After all, I'm a reporter, without political ambition, and certainly don't propose to go home and do propaganda."[93]

That may have been a bit disingenuous. Murrow was intensely political and he wanted to help the British cause, whatever the label that was attached to his work. His credibility, however, was enhanced by his being on the scene. Using the CBS airwaves from London would be far more effective than speaking in auditoriums in America.

He was heartened by Hopkins's pragmatic approach to meeting Britain's needs and by other evidence of Roosevelt's incremental moves toward providing more aid. But Murrow's doubts about American commitment remained, fueled partly by reports from colleagues who were back in America. One, Bill Shirer, wrote to Murrow that, "The ignorance of this country about its enemy is titanic." Vincent Sheean told Murrow that American news organizations veered between defeatism and wishful thinking. He said one U.S. magazine's appraisal of the future was such that it had asked him to write a lengthy account of the upcoming German march into London. Other publications, said Sheean, were understating the enormous punishment Britain was taking while overrating the impact of British bombing raids on Germany. Murrow replied, "When the American papers come in, or when I listen to American broadcasts, I am almost overcome with the desire to be ill."[94]

Murrow's passion was genuine. This distinguished him from many other correspondents who accepted the norm of detachment, which is rooted partly in the desire to remain objective and partly in world-weary cynicism. The debate about how involved journalists should be in the events they cover—whether they should practice a "journalism of commitment"—continues today. Murrow's personal views made him more susceptible to frustration, as his colleagues knew. Vincent Sheean wrote, "He was fiercely in earnest about the war, fiercely impatient with sham, incompetence, and muddle." Eric Sevareid said: "He was a great moralist, you know. He expected individuals, and his government, to live up to high moral standards. He believed in a kind of foreign policy based, I think, on moral principles, which few people really believe in any more." And Charles Collingwood said, "Besides truth, which to him was a constant object of pursuit, there are things that sound awfully big and windy, but things like honor—very important to him, his personal honor, his country's honor, and concepts like that—made his heart beat faster."[95]

These characteristics shaped Murrow's broadcasts, particularly when the horrors of the blitz infused his work with added urgency. Alexander Kendrick wrote that he "created with his words and voice a spoken Goya etching of suffering and courage." Sheean observed that Murrow lived in the homes of his listeners and through his nightly broadcasts was "like part of the evening meal, as indispensable as a knife and fork." Murrow was cautious in using radio's power, said Sheean, but "there was sometimes a world of significance in the turn of a phrase, the accent of the voice."[96]

Objectivity, if defined as emotional neutrality, is particularly slippery when the emotional content of the story is high. As 1940 drew to a close, Murrow was still prowling London's streets, touched by what he saw and heard. He noted the absence of children; most had been evacuated but many had been killed. Before the war, there had been 450,000 schoolchildren in London. By December 1940, there were only 80,400.[97] Two days before Christmas, he reported that he had listened to Christmas carols as he walked past the entrance to an air-raid shelter: "The singing was steady and firm and it came from underground." As he signed off on Christmas Eve, he said, "Merry Christmas is somehow ill-timed and out of place, so I shall just use the current London phrase—so long and good luck."[98] (He used a similar phrase, "Good night and good luck," to close his television reports in later years.)

On December 29, CBS aired a year-end roundtable discussion with Murrow as one of the commentators. He used the occasion to reiterate his feelings about America's significance and his admiration for the British people. "A year ago today," he said, "you would have found few people in Britain willing to admit that American action would determine the outcome of this war, but today the realization is widespread.... Britishers have seen a powerful enemy advance almost to their very homes and fail to dare invasion. They've seen the beginning of great social changes and have faced death in the streets and by their firesides. They have been grim and gay, true to their traditions, and they will not act otherwise in 1941."

Two nights later, he closed out the year with a sharp prod to his American listeners. His message was strong, his point of view clear: "Most of you are probably preparing to welcome the New Year. May you have a pleasant evening. You will have no dawn raid as we shall probably have if the weather is right. You may walk this night in the light. Your families are not scattered by the winds of war.... You have not been promised blood and toil and tears and sweat, and yet it is the opinion of nearly every informed observer over here that the decisions you take will overshadow all else during this year that opened an hour ago in London."[99]

By its end, 1941 was to prove to be the turning point in the war, as America's reluctance to act was overtaken by events. In March, CBS asked Murrow to devote a Sunday broadcast to a summing up of the current state of affairs. He understood that Roosevelt's stepped-up pace of providing aid was matched by Britain's growing dependence on that aid. Although he was fond of telling his listeners that "no mere radio reporter has the right to use the weight of monopolized opportunity" to influence policy, there could not be much doubt about what Murrow thought

America's policy should be. "The course of Anglo-American relations will be smooth on the surface," he said, "but many people over here will express regret because they believe America is making the same mistakes that Britain made. . . . British statesmen are fond of repeating that Britain stands alone as the defender of democracy and decency, but general headquarters is now on Pennsylvania Avenue in Washington, D.C. Many Britishers realize that; not all of them are happy about it."

Setting policy matters aside, he closed his report with another tribute to the resolve of average Britons: "During a blinding raid, when the streets are filled with smoke and the sound of roaring guns, they'll say to you, 'Do you think we're really brave, or just lacking in imagination?' Well, they've come through the winter and they've been warned that the testing days are ahead. Of the past months they may well say, 'We've lived a life, not an apology.' And of the future, I think most of them would say, 'We shall live hard, but we shall live.'"[100]

Those comments reflected Murrow's affection for the British and his tough realism about the state of the war. During wartime, thoughts inevitably turn to the future as a way to partially escape the harsh present. In the days ahead, special partnerships between Britons and Americans—Murrow among them—would increasingly shape the two nations' future.

------------------------------ Chapter **4** ------------------------------

Yanks and Brits

By the early months of 1941, life in London had settled into the syncopated rhythm of daily routine interrupted irregularly by air raids. As Hitler shifted his attention to Russia, attacks on Britain diminished, but on the war's battlegrounds there was no letup in the slog of combat.

Enduring the most intense period of the blitz had fortified Britons' spirits, and with Neville Chamberlain's death from cancer in November 1940, the era of appeasement was consigned to the past once and for all. Churchill was gracious in eulogizing his predecessor: "It fell to Neville Chamberlain in one of the supreme crises of the world to be contradicted by events, to be disappointed in his hopes, and to be deceived and cheated by a wicked man." Nevertheless, said Churchill, the former prime minister had retained "the most noble and benevolent instincts of the human heart" as shown in his ill-fated pursuit of peace.[1]

Although Murrow and most Londoners had more or less adapted to life under siege, the ferocity of the war remained stunning, particularly to those getting their first look at it. One night during an attack, Murrow stood on his rooftop with an RAF pilot who had been on many missions over Berlin but had never been on the receiving end of a raid. The young man was appalled and shaken, said he had never dreamed it was like this, and wanted only to get out of London and back into his airplane.[2]

Meanwhile, in the Murrow apartment downstairs, people had

a good time when the bombs were not too close. British politicians and BBC staff members came by to drink Ed's bourbon, laugh at his imitations of British military officials, and listen to him talk about the American Civil War and read James Thurber stories. One of his BBC guests recalled, "He was a good reader, very good, and of course it was nice to hear Thurber read in American."[3]

Elsewhere in town, the rich and famous were getting by. With heavy concrete between floors, the Dorchester Hotel was thought by some to be London's safest building. The foreign minister, Lord Halifax, had eight rooms and a private chapel there, and two stories below ground was a relatively luxurious shelter furnished with upholstered chairs and sofas that were occupied during raids by the likes of King Zog of Albania.[4] Certain conventions of society remained unchanged even in the midst of the bombing. The writer H. G. Wells was at a luncheon hosted by Lady Sibyl Colefax when German bombs started dropping nearby. His hostess suggested they adjourn to the shelter, but Wells said: "I refuse to go to the shelter until I have had my cheese. I'm enjoying a very good lunch. Why should I be disturbed by some wretched little barbarian adolescents in a machine. This thing has no surprises for me. I foresaw it long ago. Sibyl, I want my cheese."[5]

Presumably Mr. Wells received and enjoyed his cheese. Like many of his countrymen, he refused to let Hitler terrify him, and as weeks and months passed, it was increasingly clear that Britain was going to be able to hang on, although only with help. Murrow was among those who fretted about America's continued refusal to enter the war, although after the 1940 election Roosevelt had significantly increased the quantity of aid to Britain.

The U.S.–U.K. relationship received daily attention in London. To fully understand the significance of Murrow's interventionist efforts, it is important to have a sense of the larger context of how information was gathered, shaped, and delivered by American and British officials who were committed to getting the United States to truly go to war.

This process could be seen in numerous venues, including

Ed and Janet Murrow, London, 1938.
Edward R. Murrow Photographs, Historical Photograph Collection, Manuscripts,
Archives and Special Collections, Washington State University.

The 30-year-old Murrow at work, January 1939. Landov.

Murrow in wartime London, 1941. The BBC building (with antennas) is in the background. Landov.

*The blitz begins, September 7, 1940, as London's docks
burn behind Tower Bridge.*
Courtesy, Franklin D. Roosevelt Library.

St. Paul's Cathedral survives a massive air raid, December 1940. Landov.

Britons carry on after a raid. Landov.

*An Underground station in London's West End becomes
the new nightly home for hundreds.*
Courtesy, Franklin D. Roosevelt Library.

Murrow returning to New York, November 1941.
Edward R. Murrow Photographs, Historical Photograph Collection, Manuscripts,
Archives and Special Collections, Washington State University.

the U.S. Embassy. Joseph Kennedy was gone, leaving behind a bitter aftertaste produced by his persistent defeatism. His replacement was a quiet Republican, a three-time governor of New Hampshire and good friend of Murrow, John Gilbert Winant.

Winant's political views developed during the days when the Republican Party had a liberal wing. A supporter of the New Deal and a proponent of social justice as an elected official, he had also been director of the International Labor Organization—a body created by the Treaty of Versailles as a non-Marxist means to improve workers' living standards—and had been appointed by Roosevelt as first chairman of the Social Security Board. He was occasionally mentioned as a prospective presidential candidate, but his popularity with journalists and non-partisan activists was partly based on his being a political outsider. One newspaper article noted that Winant smiled easily, "like a human being, rather than a politician."[6]

His reputation as a compassionate liberal won him endorsements for the ambassador's post. British political theorist Harold Laski wrote to an American friend, "Send us John Winant as ambassador and, even more, secure the permanent end of Joe Kennedy's political career." Murrow, who in political outlook and personal temperament had much in common with Winant, urged the White House to appoint him. When that happened, he wrote to Winant, "This is indeed good news."[7]

Initial British reaction was cautiously positive. *The Times* observed that Winant was "a man slow to reach a decision but inflexible when convinced and today as fully awake to the tremendous moral and social issues of the conflict of which he will be a spectator as anyone alive. Britons will discover they are dealing with a man in whom confidences can be placed unhesitatingly."[8] A Foreign Office memorandum described Winant as "exceedingly shy and very earnest. . . difficult in small talk" but has a "sense of social service which amounts almost to religious conviction." Some conservative British officials looked askance at Winant's reformist credentials and noted that stalwart New Dealer Ben Cohen would join the new ambassador as his legal advisor. They wondered if this was a sign that Roosevelt had it in mind to foster a "social revolution" in Britain. Rebutting this notion, Foreign Office official T. North Whitehead (son of philosopher Alfred North Whitehead) wrote, "Mr. Roosevelt is not Lenin and it is highly improbable that he would attempt to interfere with our internal politics."[9]

Just before departing for London, Winant was told by Roosevelt that "he wanted me to keep Winston Churchill and the British government patient while the American people assessed the issues which faced them." Winant was to work carefully at this task, but he left no doubt about his own sympathies. In a farewell speech to the New Hampshire legislature, he said: "Great Britain has asked that we give them the tools that they may 'finish the job.' We can stand with them as free men in the comradeship of hard work, not asking but giving, with unity of purpose in defense of liberty under law, of government answerable to the people."[10]

Winant was busy from the moment he arrived in Britain. He flew into Bristol on March 1, 1941 and told reporters at the airport, "There is no place I would rather be at this time than in England." From there, he went by train to Windsor, where King George awaited him at the railway station—the first time in history that a British monarch had gone to meet an ambassador. (The king made this gesture in part to reciprocate for Roosevelt having traveled to Annapolis to greet the new British ambassador, Lord Halifax, who arrived on Britain's newest battleship.)[11]

Churchill was eager to talk to Winant as soon as he arrived. The first order of business was to implement the Lend-Lease program concocted by Roosevelt. Winant later wrote, "It is probably true that no act of a neutral power ever contributed more to the defeat of an aggressor nation." Nevertheless, rough spots still needed to be smoothed out. Churchill's private secretary John Colville noted that Britain's West Indian colonies were not enthusiastic about ninety-nine-year leases being granted to the United States and resented "conditions which the Americans have demanded and which amount to capitulations." Churchill, however, worked with Winant to override such objections, stating that "the safety of the state is at stake" and that the American aid "will enable us to win the war, which we could otherwise not do."[12]

Winant recognized that in addition to helping Churchill he also had to deal with American isolationist pressure, and so in speeches he noted that Congress, when approving the Lend-Lease legislation, had stated that "This Act may be cited as 'An Act to promote the defense of the United States.'" He stepped up his advocacy of American involvement in speeches that had much in common with the message Murrow was sending to his U.S. audience but that carried the presumed endorsement of Roosevelt. A week after his arrival in London, he said, "In the struggle against the Nazis the people of Britain hold the front line, but they do not stand isolated and alone." America, he said, "is mobilizing with ever-growing speed its tremendous resources to make available to you the sinews of war." He took an even stronger position in another speech: "When clever, cunning dictators are striking with lightning speed at any and every free nation that dares stand in their way, the time has come for democratic nations to prove to the world that, while they are free to debate, they have the power and the will to act. . . . We have made our tasks infinitely more difficult because we failed to do yesterday what we gladly do today. Much that we do today would not have been necessary had we done enough yesterday. The longer the delay, the more protracted will be the war, and the greater the sacrifices which will be required for victory."[13]

When Murrow delivered such a message, British officials were pleased by just the words themselves and the effect on U.S. opinion that they might have. But from Winant, words were not enough. If his hawkish pronouncements truly represented the feelings of the American president, then the United States should be expected to back them up with greater participation in the war effort.

While Winant sought firm footing on his difficult diplomatic terrain, he forged a close relationship with Winston Churchill. The prime minister liked Winant well enough personally, but he also recognized that the new ambassador—in contrast to his predecessor—could provide useful backchannels into the American policymaking hierarchy and advance the British agenda. For his part, Winant admired Churchill and the others in the war cabinet "who had first sensed danger and who had determined to meet it." These men, wrote Winant, "gave me their confidence because they knew I believed in their cause and in their will and ability to defend that cause, even while they stood alone." His efforts as diplomat paralleled those of Murrow as broadcaster. Neither had real power to shape policy, but they could reach those who did, and both men were fervent believers in the rightness of the British cause. They also both believed—and would make clear to all who would listen—that Britain would fight on and, with American help, would prevail.

Winant kept Washington informed about individual British officials' attitudes toward American policy. "In my opinion," he wrote, "one of the most important elements in international relations is to know who the true friends of your country are in other governments and to do what can be done to make their trust and confidence a help to them in their effort to establish good relationships."[14] At the top of his list of the true friends was Churchill, who lobbied Winant constantly at Downing Street and during weekends at Chequers. After only three months in Britain, Winant went back to Washington at the behest of the prime minister to urge—successfully, as it turned out—that American officials relieve some of the pressure on Britain by extending U.S. Navy patrols farther into the Western Atlantic and taking over the protection of Iceland.[15]

Winant had seen Churchill in action in bombed-out Swansea and Bristol and wrote to Roosevelt to describe the prime minister's way of boosting morale: "He arrives at a town unannounced, is taken to the most seriously bombed area, leaves his automobile, and starts walking through the streets without guards. The news of his presence spreads rapidly by word of mouth, and before he has gone far, crowds flock about him and people call out to him, 'Hallo, Winnie,' 'Good old Winnie,' 'You will never let us down,'

'That's a man.' I was interested to note that his 'Cheerio' in our earlier visits changed to 'God bless you' when we reached Bristol where people were still shaken by the bombing. The whole town was back on its feet again and cheering within two hours of his arrival, although no one had got any sleep during the night."[16]

Winant also became a close friend of Foreign Secretary Anthony Eden. The two would sometimes escape to Eden's Sussex home on weekends, where, wrote Winant, "We used to get our fun weeding the garden. We would put our dispatch boxes at either end, and when we had completed a row we would do penance by reading messages and writing the necessary replies. Then we would start again our menial task, each in some subconscious fashion trying to find a sense of lasting values in the good earth."[17] Eden said of Winant, "He cares much for his work, little for party politics, not at all for himself." The two worked in tandem so well, wrote Eden, "that we could agree together which parts of our conversations should be on the record for the information of our two governments and which for ourselves alone."[18]

Most other British officials with whom Winant dealt also liked him. BBC governor Harold Nicolson said, "Winant is one of the most charming men that I have ever met. He has emphatic eyes and an unemphatic voice." Churchill's private secretary John Colville called him "a gentle, dreamy idealist, whom most men and all women loved."[19] Colville admired his work as ambassador and told of the time that he had taken a draft of a Churchill speech to Winant, who immediately read it and "made four pertinent observations in respect of the effect on U.S. opinion and I was deeply impressed by his unassertive shrewdness and wisdom. . . . While I was with the ambassador a blitz started. He did not even raise his head." Colville added that Churchill accepted Winant's suggestions.[20]

There were, however, mixed reviews of his performance as ambassador. Critics said he was inefficient in keeping to his schedule and did not maintain good communication within the embassy. Ministry of Information official Ronald Tree said Winant was "a loner" and "full of idiosyncrasies." Tree added that "late at night he would turn up at the house of one of his close friends [sometimes Murrow's] and would walk up and down the sitting room, inveighing against some supposed slight he had received at the hands of the president or [Lend-Lease administrator] Averill Harriman. His hours of work and way of transacting business drove his staff to near despair." But even Tree observed, "In Winant Britain had a true and trusted friend."[21]

Such friendship can create problems because managing dual loyalties is difficult. Winant, like Murrow, seemed able to maintain an appropriate balance. Churchill later said that Winant had never become an Anglophile to the extent of compromising his role as the representative of the American government. He put Britain's efforts, said Churchill, "in the best light before the American people, and yet would still do it as a patriotic American."[22]

Churchill and his colleagues may have liked Winant because he was a useful advocate for their cause, but the key factor in Winant's popularity with the British public was his behavior during the bombing raids on London. During an attack in April 1941 that shattered the U.S. embassy's windows and did heavy damage to the surrounding neighborhood, Winant walked through the nearby streets, asking if there was any way he could help. He wasn't needed to remove victims of the raid or fight the fires, but he stayed on the scene until dawn, when people emerging from the shelters saw him heading back to the embassy. The news media picked up the story and Winant's reputation was established throughout the country. He later wrote about those nights under attack, saying that "to those of us in the embassy in this period, it made the war real, for it gave us a feeling of sharing with the men and women who worked so untiringly in Britain's ordeal to survive." In a letter to Roosevelt, he said: "There are two things which have impressed me most: The first, the effort to maintain the appearance of normal life in the face of danger, and the second, the patient acceptance of hardships and hazards by ordinary people."[23]

❋   ❋   ❋   ❋

On July 4, 1941, some Londoners flew American flags from their rooftops and Winant attended a memorial service at St. Paul's Cathedral for Billy Fiske, an American who had talked his way into the RAF and had been killed in a dogfight with German planes. A memorial tablet in the cathedral crypt identified Fiske as "An American citizen who died that England might live."

Beyond symbolic gestures, Winant wanted Britons to get a good look at America and he hoped that the British press would expand its coverage of the United States. But, he noted, "The shortage of labor in the printing trade and the limited supply of paper reduced the size of the British newspapers to four pages. This further restricted the coverage of news from the United States." To partly offset this, the BBC carried news commentaries from American broadcasters such as Raymond Gram Swing and Elmer Davis. Winant understood the power of information, but despite his friendship with Murrow and other journalists, he was skeptical about the quality of reporting. After a supposedly private meeting with Vice President Henry Wallace and several senators during one of his trips to Washington, he found stories about the session the next day in two New York newspapers, one with a headline proclaiming, "Winant Reports Britain Thinks Victory Certain," and the other, "British Position Extremely Grave But Not Disastrous, Winant Says." "I could only hope," wrote Winant, "that the conflicting nature of the articles might in some measure confuse the enemy."[24]

If Winant was frustrated with the news media, Murrow was increasingly impatient with what he considered to be U.S. foot-dragging. In Winant, Murrow found the passionate commitment that he shared and that he yearned to see in America's political leaders. He wrote to Winant: "I have unbounded admiration for the job you are doing. If some time in the unpredictable future you decide to go home and seek political power, I may be one of the 'goodly company' to travel with you."[25]

Murrow never had the opportunity to help his friend politically, as Winant came to a sad end. After his mentor Franklin Roosevelt died and the war concluded, he was overwhelmed by professional and personal frustrations. He left the ambassador-ship and was appointed by President Harry Truman to a United Nations post, but that job left Winant fighting bureaucratic battles rather than helping to build a better post-war world. He completed a volume of memoirs about his first year as ambassador, but writing was a terrible ordeal for him. Facing substantial debts and feeling hopelessly alone, he committed suicide in November 1947 at age fifty-eight.

In a foreword to a posthumously published collection of Winant's speeches, Winston Churchill wrote that the ambassador had "won for himself the respect and admiration of the whole British nation. Mr. Winant always put the American point of view with force and clarity, and argued his country's cause with the utmost vigor, but his constant purpose was to smooth away the difficulties and prevent any misunderstandings, and he always gave us the feeling of how gladly he would give his life to see the good cause triumph. He was a friend of Britain, but he was more than a friend of Britain. He was a friend of justice, freedom, and truth."[26]

❋   ❋   ❋   ❋

While Churchill was exhorting Winant to keep pressure on Roosevelt, the Ministry of Information and the BBC were considering ways that Murrow might become even more effective as a voice for British interests. Murrow continued to be agreeable to appearing on BBC broadcasts as his schedule allowed, and his scripts were carefully scrutinized by BBC officials. One BBC memorandum noted that an upcoming Murrow talk included some tart comments about U.S. policy and said, "I would like to keep his vigorous criticisms of some things American, which would come ill from an Englishman but I hope we can pass them from an American." But sometimes overeager BBC officials mis-used Murrow's words. A memo warned that a "bad blunder" had been made when comments by Murrow were taken out of context and advertised by the BBC as being a political response to isolationist statements by former president Herbert Hoover.

For the most part, however, the relationship proceeded smoothly, with Murrow doing special programs—such as fifteen-minute "Meet Uncle Sam" broadcasts—to explain America to Britons. He also reviewed content and joined discussions about the United States for the "Radio Reconnaissance" program, which was broadcast to British troops. BBC officials noted that Murrow's participation in such programs about America was important because he would "show how that country, in spite of the superficial resemblances it bears to our own, must be looked at afresh if we are to understand it, and of course it is more important now than at any time in history that we should understand it."[27]

By mid-1941, the BBC was developing plans for an elaborate broadcast to air if and when the United States declared war, and Murrow met with BBC officials to discuss the content. He would be featured in the special program, which would also include inspiring music such as "The Battle Hymn of the Republic" and "Hope and Glory."[28]

Although he helped with such projects, Murrow kept the pressure on British information officials to allow him more access to the people and events he wanted to cover. He clearly expected a quid pro quo for his assistance and sometimes his impatience with British bureaucracy flared, as when an Admiralty public information officer complained that Murrow had not provided enough information in a request to accompany a naval convoy. Murrow told BBC liaison officer Roger Eckersley, "I have not the least sympathy for the overworked public relations officer at the Admiralty, particularly since I have just finished about six weeks of night work for the Admiralty, doing a commentary for a film which is going to the States."[29]

The British had to pay attention to Murrow's complaints because they needed his help in offsetting the still potent isolationist sentiment in America. Charles Lindbergh continued to attract large supportive crowds to his anti-intervention speeches. *Time* magazine reported that at an America First rally in Chicago in April 1941, mention of Churchill drew boos and "when Colonel Lindbergh said that England was in a desperate situation, her shipping losses serious, 'her cities devastated by bombs,' he was stopped—and embarrassed—by applause."[30]

Taking note of such reports, British officials looked for still more ways to win over American journalists. Even the royal family was enlisted in this effort. David Bowes-Lyon, the Queen's brother and chief of the press section of the Ministry of Economic Warfare, arranged an afternoon party so his sister could meet American correspondents whom he knew from his job. Journalist Vincent Sheean wrote that each reporter was taken to sit beside the queen for a one-on-one chat of about five minutes, and although each approached her with a rather worried look, "each in turn thawed under the influence of her simple, friendly charm; and each one, when he got up, was smiling and conquered. . . . I thought her candid eyes and touchingly pure voice (an almost childlike voice) did more to disarm us all, if we needed disarming, than any amount of splendor might have done."[31]

With their visits to bombed-out neighborhoods and other public appearances, the royal family was an invaluable asset in maintaining domestic morale as well as winning sympathy overseas. Ed and Janet Murrow were among the Americans in London who were invited to Buckingham Palace to partake of pomp and charm. But such occasions were rare, and American journalists had much more contact with middle-tier British officials such as Harold Nicolson.

✻   ✻   ✻   ✻

Like Churchill, whom he admired greatly, Nicolson was one of those renaissance men of public life that Britain has produced over the years. Born in 1886, he entered the diplomatic service as a young man, was posted to Istanbul and Berlin, and participated in the victors' redrawing of national boundaries in 1919. He admitted then that "my courage fails at the thought of the people whom our errant lines enclose or exclude."[32] He wrote articles for the *Spectator* and authored thirty-five books ranging from a biography of Tennyson to a study of the Congress of Vienna. He also spent a decade in Parliament, and said that although he did not have the "lust for battle" necessary to become a parliamentary leader, "I love the House since I am a sociable person and much enjoy observing the oddities of my fellow beings. I find the House rather like one of those marine diving-bells in which one can sit and watch the vagaries of the deep-sea fish."[33]

As war approached, he was part of the Conservatives' anti-Chamberlain caucus in which Ronald Tree was also active. He feared that when Hitler finally moved against Poland, Chamberlain would back down from his agreement to protect the Poles and be cheered at home as "the Great Appeaser." When the war began, he was asked by a publisher to write a book about the reasons for fighting. He wrote the 50,000-word *Why England Is at War* in two weeks and when the book went on sale in November 1939, 5,000 copies a day had to be printed to keep up with demand.[34] He set forth a lofty and compelling argument in support of Britain's belated decision to confront Hitler. "We entered this war," he wrote, "to defend ourselves. We shall continue to, to its most bitter end, in order to save humanity." The sudden shift from appeasement to war had left many Britons confused. "The British people at the present moment," wrote Nicolson, "are disheartened by the fact that they do not know what they are fighting for. . . . The time will come, of course (and it will come with thunder and fire), when the British people will realize that they are fighting for their very existence."[35]

Murrow shared Nicolson's anti-appeasement feelings and quoted from Nicolson's *Spectator* articles when he wanted to get opinions that he agreed with on the air. The two men differed, however, in their appraisals of Londoners' staying power. Historian Philip Ziegler has pointed out that Nicolson tended to underestimate British fortitude. Nicolson wrote during the blitz that "the spirit of London is excellent, but it would take little to swing this country into cowardice," and "one cannot expect the population of a great city to sit up all night in shelters week after week without losing their spirit." He also wrote, "I think that we can resist the worst, but we shall be so exhausted by that resistance

that Hitler may offer us an honorable peace which will be difficult to reject."[36] Nicolson was simply wrong about that. People
may have become exhausted and depressed, but there is no evidence that there was any substantial sentiment to quit.

Nicolson's evaluations of the state of affairs varied and he
sometimes set aside at least some of his pessimism: "We are conscious all the time that this is a moment in history. But it is very
like falling down a mountain. One is aware of death and fate, but
thinks mainly of catching hold of some jutting piece of rock. I
have a sense of strain and unhappiness, but none of fear. One
feels so proud."[37]

One topic on which Nicolson and Murrow agreed absolutely was Joseph Kennedy. Nicolson wrote that after a high-level
meeting in December 1940, most of the conversation was about
"Joe Kennedy and his treachery to us and Roosevelt. The general
idea is that he will do harm for the moment but not in the end.
How right I was in warning people against him. I was the first to
do so."[38]

Another person angered by Kennedy's pronouncements was
Churchill, whom Nicolson observed closely. His sketches of the
war leader provide a good sense of the charismatic forcefulness
that won him the allegiance of Britons, the trust of Roosevelt,
and the admiration of Murrow. Nicolson described a dinner party
at which American journalist Walter Lippmann told Churchill that
Kennedy was spreading the word that the British were sure to
lose the war. Churchill, wrote Nicolson, was "stirred by this defeatism into a magnificent oration," telling Lippmann that no
matter how bad things became, "dire peril and fierce ordeals"
would "serve to steel the resolution of the British people and to
enhance our will for victory." If Britain should be defeated, said
Churchill, "it will then be for you, the Americans, to preserve
and to maintain the great heritage of the English-speaking
peoples. It will be for you to think imperially, which means to
think always of something higher and more vast than one's own
national interests. Nor should I die happy in the great struggle
which I see before me were I not convinced that if we in this dear

dear island succumb to the ferocity and might of our enemies, over there in your distant and immune continent the torch of liberty will burn untarnished and, I trust and hope, undismayed." Not bad for dinner table conversation. (Then, wrote Nicolson, "we change the subject and speak about the Giant Panda.")[39]

During the early days of the war, Nicolson noted the contrast between Chamberlain and Churchill. During an uninspiring House of Commons speech by Chamberlain, Churchill "sat hunched beside him looking like the Chinese god of plenty suffering from acute indigestion." When Churchill then spoke, the effect "was infinitely greater than could be derived from any reading of the text. His delivery was really amazing and he sounded every note from deep preoccupation to flippancy, from resolution to sheer boyishness. One could feel the spirits of the House rising with every word." And after Churchill later delivered his "We shall fight on the beaches" speech, Nicolson wrote, "I feel so much in the spirit of Winston's great speech that I could face a world of enemies."[40]

Appointed by Churchill as parliamentary secretary at the Ministry of Information during Alfred Duff Cooper's tenure, Nicolson provided Murrow a sympathetic ear within a bureaucracy that frustrated so many journalists. While reporters saw MoI as an obstruction, the public also disliked the ministry because of its patronizing and unrealistic sunniness. Nicolson's biographer James Lees-Milne observed that beyond a detachment from reality, part of MoI's problem was that "seldom have so many literary intellectuals been assembled under one roof."[41] This produced plenty of controversy and infighting, which sometimes took precedence over the commitment to increase the flow of information. Nicolson tried to keep the ministry on track, arguing that uninformative war communiqués "must be altered and we cannot possibly starve the public in this way."

He also knew that coming up with a helpful message was difficult when the war was going badly, as it was in mid-1940. He wrote that "all the country really wants is some assurance of how victory is to be achieved. They are bored by talks about the righteousness of our cause and our eventual triumph. What they want are facts indicating how we are to beat the Germans. I have no idea at all how we are to give them those facts."[42]

Nicolson understood the limitations inherent in trying to deliver honest propaganda. Therefore, he wrote, "it may be true that if our propaganda is to be as effective as that of the enemy, we must have at top people who will not only command the assent of the press, but who will be caddish and ignorant enough to tell dynamic lies. At present the Ministry is too decent, educated, and intellectual to imitate Goebbels." Despite his concerns about the effectiveness of the British message, he stopped short of embracing Goebbels's approach. He wrote in the *BBC Handbook* that "totalitarian methods of propaganda are not only foolish as such but wholly inapplicable to a civilized community. . . . No permanent propaganda policy can in the modern world be based upon untruthfulness."[43]

Despite the requirements of wartime information management, Nicolson appreciated the value of truth, which could not be said of everyone in the official information business, and so remained an ally of Murrow and other journalists. Beyond that, he was one of those rare political figures—Churchill was another—who proved that literary sensibilities and a commitment to public service need not be mutually exclusive. His diaries and letters, published years later, reflected this. He wrote, for instance, in April 1939 about working with his wife, Vita Sackville-West, in their country garden, planting annuals: "We rake the soil smooth. And as we rake we are both thinking, 'What will have happened to the world when these seeds germinate?'" With the war underway, his writings were imbued with a mix of hope and sadness, as when he observed that "the whole of Europe [is] humiliated except us" and that there was "the chance that we shall by our stubbornness give victory to the world."

During the grim days when London was first being bombed, he wrote: "One lives in the present. The past is too sad a recollection and the future too sad a despair." As Britain continued to fight and survive, his spirits rose: "One's patriotism, which has been a vague family feeling, is now a flame in the night. I may have felt arrogant about the British Empire in past years; today I feel quite humbly proud of the British people."[44]

❋   ❋   ❋   ❋

Although Murrow also felt proud of the British people and championed them in his broadcasts to his huge American audience, his influence had its limits. What power he had was unofficial and indirect, affecting U.S. policy only when ripples of public opinion reached politically sensitive officials. Even then, policymakers could count on the public's attention span being short.

A shrewd politician such as Franklin Roosevelt understood the transient nature of pro-British blips in popular sentiment stimulated by Murrow or others. When he formulated policy, he relied on his official family—advisors in Washington and those reporting from London. Some, such as Harry Hopkins, have become well known. One of the most influential, however, has been overlooked by many historians. He was a brigadier general and the military attaché at the American Embassy on Grosvenor Square, whose cool judgments of military and political affairs were valued highly by Roosevelt. His appraisals of Britain's prospects gave the president a foundation on which to build his plans for assisting Churchill.

Raymond E. Lee was born in St. Louis in 1886 and graduated from the University of Missouri with a degree in civil engineering. He decided to make the Army his career and worked his way up the military ladder: he was an artillery commander at Verdun during World War I and served in the Philippines, at the National War College, and in other postings before being assigned to London in 1935. By the time the war began, he was well established in the U.K., with many close contacts in the upper echelons of British military and civilian officialdom. He was, for example, friendly with Nancy Astor in her post-appeasement years and was a frequent guest at Cliveden, where he hobnobbed with politicians, journalists, and celebrities such as George Bernard Shaw. When the blitz began, Lee, like many of his British colleagues, took his steel helmet to an upscale Jermyn Street hatter to be fitted with a comfortable lining.[45]

Lee kept a detailed journal, an abridged version of which was published after his death in 1958. It provides a superb look not only at London life and politics but also at the work of a senior intelligence officer. This was not cloak-and-dagger espionage, but rather the gathering and gleaning of information from diverse sources, ranging from British officials to journalists to wandering émigrés. His journal entries include information that was sent to Washington and ended up on the president's desk. FDR valued appraisals from insiders with first-hand knowledge of people and events, which made Lee's reports so influential. In October 1940, the president told a visiting British general that for fast and accurate information he relied on two primary sources: material provided by British ambassador Lord Lothian and cables from Raymond Lee.[46]

Roosevelt probably would have enjoyed Lee's personal observations, which were not in his cables but remained in his journal. He often made tart comments about some of those he worked with. From his vantage point at the embassy, Lee had a good view of the machinations of Ambassador Kennedy, who, Lee observed, "has the speculator's smartness but also [a] sharpshooting and facile insensitivity to the great forces which are now playing like heat lightning over the map of the world." In another entry, Lee described Kennedy as "crude, blatant, and ignorant in everything he did or said."[47]

During the first days of the blitz in 1940, Lee was caught up in the mix of bravery and fatalism that pervaded London. He wrote, "If ever there was a time when one should wear life like a loose garment, this is it," and when more antiaircraft guns were committed to the fight in October, he observed, "It is difficult to express how enchanting the roar of these big guns is to the dwellers in London." He did not hear complaints from Londoners, just softly spoken requests for support. A seamstress said to him, "If you could only tell your countrymen how much we need their help to survive." There never was panic, and Lee noted the "fine, dignified self-control about the British when they are in trouble and tossed about."[48]

Lee lived at Claridge's, a luxury hotel near the embassy that had plenty of rooms available because of the bombing. Lee thought the building's steel frame made it as strong as any structure and was pleased to accept the manager's offer of a fourth floor corner suite for $7.50 a day. (He was offered the penthouse for free, but decided that living at rooftop level might be pressing his luck.)

Lee was one of the most persistent advocates for the proposition that Britain, with a decent amount of help from the United States, could win the war. He grounded his opinion not in wishful thinking but in hardheaded judgments about British military capabilities, particularly in the air. During Kennedy's tenure as ambassador, Lee's voice was important in offsetting pronouncements from the pessimists. One British journalist told Lee, "You are the only one in the embassy who has had courage enough to speak his mind about England's winning this war," a role which was "well known in the highest quarters in London."[49]

Lee was summoned to Washington for about three months in early 1941 to participate in talks among military leaders of the United States, Britain, and Canada. This lengthy conference developed plans for coordination should America enter the war. After returning to London in April, Lee sensed that the British were being worn down: "I think I notice a considerable deterioration in many directions, which I might possibly not have noticed had I not been away. There is no question but that the food situation is very much worse. The people strike me also as being much more solemn than they were in January." He recommended that more U.S. officials come to Britain because "it is only by being here that one realizes the actuality and the pressure of the emergency."[50]

British officials presented Lee with the same basic argument for help that they used with Murrow and other American journalists. Lee noted in his journal that the consistent message was that "the British cannot win without our assistance and this assistance must come in a hurry and in great quantity." Much of Lee's support for prompt American aid was based on his belief that the United States would be hard pressed if it had to face Hitler after Britain had fallen. "One thing is certain," he wrote, "if this country is knocked out, we will have to stand alone and will have a hard time doing it." Lee despaired about what he called the "pathetic apathy" in America and wrote that it was "the same sort of apathy which has led to the overthrow of so many other nations and which really is the thing that Hitler has taken great advantage of." He cited approvingly an editorial in *The Times* of London that said about Americans, "It is time these people realize they are living on earth and not in the clouds."[51]

Lee paid particular attention to the flow of information from the British government and the journalists who put that information to work. In his capacity as the embassy's intelligence chief, he provided officials in Washington with a steady stream of analyses based on information that was in the public domain—such as news reports—and material that he gathered privately at high-toned Mayfair dinner parties and from casual conversations with reporters.

He also monitored American news coverage of Britain. During the first weeks of the blitz, he expressed concern about sensational photographs in *Life* and *Time* that showed wounded children, raging fires, and the like. He worried that although such photos would elicit sympathy they might also make Britain appear doomed and not worth helping. Similarly, he took issue with coverage in the *New York Times,* which featured headlines such as these: "Nazis Pound London in All-day Raids; Bomb Northwest City for Six Hours"; "Nazis Raid Britain in Waves"; "1,500 Nazi Planes Bomb London; Industry and Services Damaged"; "Mighty Nazi Air Fleet Again Bombs London—Docks and Plants Hit, Fires Rage, 400 Dead." The headlines were accurate, but Lee pointed out that there was a larger picture—life in London was proceeding. "The fact is," he wrote, "that many of the American papers are dressed up till one would almost imagine we are groping from one street corner to another with shells and bombs falling like rain. I suppose the public demands sensational terms, but if the *New York Times* prints such stuff, what must be appearing in the cheap press!" Concerned about the political impact of the coverage, he said that he had "tacked a paragraph onto my cable to say that morale was very high in spite of the apprehensions raised in some people's breasts together with the actual lack of sleep."[52]

Murrow avoided overstating the damage done by the German raids and made clear that Londoners were persevering. But Lee wanted to make a point to some of the other American journalists. *New York Times* correspondent James Reston was among the reporters Lee asked to come to his office one day during the blitz. Years later, Reston recalled that Lee had a big dictionary on his desk and said to the journalists, "I notice that some of you are writing that London is 'devastated.' In my dictionary that means 'laid waste, ravaged, demolished.' Please, gentlemen, don't make it worse than it is."[53]

Lee also tried to steer other American journalists' reporting, with mixed results. Columnist Dorothy Thompson was intent on describing the burdens of the British war effort as being borne exclusively by "the common people." Although Lee told her that she was wrong and pointed out the contributions and sacrifices of members of the upper classes, Thompson wrote the column. Lee noted in his journal: "I thought she was very stupid to have done so." He had friendlier conversations with *Washington Post* owner Eugene Meyer, who had come to London for a first-hand look, and Lee made himself available to American reporters who needed an escort to examine British coastal fortifications.[54]

As he read stories in the American press about U.S. public opinion, Lee became concerned about the growing popularity of armed isolationism—the position that the best course for the United States was to stay out of the war but bolster its ability to defend itself. "Evidently," wrote Lee, "all the emphasis which has been placed on defense, defense, defense has robbed the American people of any desire to go out and hit the Germans on the head. If we are going to keep the idea of waiting at home until they come over after us, we will find that they will not do it until the British have been disposed of and then we will be single-handed and in a damn bad fix."[55] This was a theme Lee addressed frequently in his journals and it inspired him to push for further cooperation with the British in devising a joint war plan. Despite such efforts by Lee and others and despite Hitler's formidable record of military success, polls indicated that Americans felt they could handle the Germans on their own should the need arise.

Lee had some success controlling British coverage of American news. When Ambassador Winant, while on a trip to the United States, was quoted inaccurately in American newspapers as saying he was very pessimistic about Britain's chances, he issued a denial and called the London embassy to ask for help in keeping the original stories out of the British press. Lee and other embassy officials were able to get the Ministry of Information to temporarily halt the printing of news cables from New York, allowing Winant's rebuttal to catch up with the initial reports.[56]

Lee also kept an eye on propaganda. He suggested to Harold Nicolson that American broadcasts from London, Berlin, Moscow, and elsewhere be made available to the British audience. Believing that the British needed to be more aggressive in using radio to demoralize their enemy, he cited the Russians, who, he said, "have suddenly shown the British what real two-fisted propaganda is. Their ingenious personal broadcasts to some individual German wife, mother, or father, whose husband or son has been found dead on the battlefield and properly identified, have a diabolical ingenuity to them which the British are not capable of evolving, at least in their present state of mind, which is that of the kid glove, public school, playing fields of Eton character."[57]

Lee understood that Americans would be more likely to support increased aid to Britain if there were harmonious relations between the British and U.S. military, and he knew that an unimpeded flow of information was essential to that relationship. He made that point clear to his British colleagues, as in this November 1940 memo: "The United States entered the last war in 1917 practically blindfolded because a great range of vital facts had been withheld from our representatives both here and in Paris. This has never been forgotten in Washington. It must not happen this time. If the full support of the United States is desired, the president and his advisers are entitled to the complete and detailed picture, whether it is favorable or not, so that they can make their decisions with their eyes open. The whole affair is now at a point at which Congress must decide whether the United States is to finance the rest of the war. If any impression gets about in Washington that any facts are being withheld on this side, so that our reports are partial, biased, or misinformed, it is going to be too bad."[58]

Along these lines, Lee kept careful watch on reporting about Britain's military capabilities. During the first weeks of the blitz, Lee was asked by the War Department in Washington about the Churchill government's claims that the British were leading the Germans in aircraft production and pilot availability. Lee answered: "They have only the vaguest estimates of German production and their pilot production is just about level with their losses." Lee added that to improve the situation the War Department should lease airfields in the United States to the British for pilot training.[59]

Lee also monitored British responses to private aid provided by Americans, such as the assistance provided by Bundles for Britain. When a friend told him that British officials had been slow to acknowledge the gift of a $100,000 mobile surgical unit, Lee was clearly irritated by the British behavior. He told his friend to go to Anthony Eden, then in the War Office, and inform him "that if the British could not have good manners about such things they might well look forward to the freely flowing American spring drying up. They do not understand in this country that it pays to advertise and they do not understand that the United States is not one of their suppliant dominions."[60]

Despite such occasional problems, Lee retained his belief in Great Britain's ability to eventually prevail in the war and he admired British persistence. In one of his journal entries, Lee said:

"What a wonderful thing it will be if these blokes do win the war! They will be bankrupt but entitled to almost unlimited respect. They are not quitters." Similarly, he understood how carefully the United States should plan for its involvement in the fighting: "We are the final reserve force of democracy. Therefore, we cannot afford to make any mistake as to where we apply our power, for when we finally conclude to strike, if that does not settle the matter finally and conclusively, the final disappearance of democracy will be foreshadowed."[61]

During summer 1941, Ambassador Winant asked Lee to prepare an assessment of the current British military situation that Winant could present to the president. Lee wrote: "The forces which Germany can exert are too enormous to be halted at once. They are like a flow of lava, irresistible and overwhelming. At the same time, like lava, I am confident that as they spread further from the volcano's mouth, they will cool and slow down. . . . I still believe the British can resist invasion. It will be a hard, bloody business. . . . I have never believed and cannot see how the British Empire can defeat Germany without the help of God or Uncle Sam. Perhaps it will take both." Harry Hopkins liked Lee's report—particularly his lava analogy—because it provided a bit of optimism at a time when optimism was in short supply. Roosevelt also welcomed encouraging words about British prospects.[62]

In London, British officials continued to appreciate Lee's importance and they treated him as an especially close colleague. Unlike other foreign military officers, he could walk into the War Office and even into the office of the chief of British Military Intelligence without a pass.

John Winant also valued Lee's advice on a wide array of matters. Lee told of the time that Winant shyly requested help in shopping for clothes: "I loaded the ambassador into my car and led him down to Scholte's, where we ordered him two suits of clothes to replace the dreadful looking garments he had been wearing. As soon as this was done, I suggested that a new hat would be in order. He has been wearing a funny-looking little felt affair, badly battered and discolored and completely out of proportion to his size and height. He fell in with the suggestion. . . and we came away with not one but two, which will make a great difference in appearance. On the way back to the office he sighed with relief and said, 'That really was easy.'"[63]

With his expertise ranging from war to wardrobe, Lee was the indispensable man at the U.S. Embassy. Part of his value was his understanding of the power of information and the importance of public opinion, and he proceeded along a path running parallel to Murrow's in terms of using information to shape opinion and policy.

More so than Murrow, Lee looked at journalism as a means to an end. He wanted news reports from London to encourage American intervention and not fuel pessimism, and he did not hesitate to push coverage in that direction whenever he had the opportunity. Lee understood that his own cables were a kind of journalism, and he also knew that his audience was small but select, principally at the War Department and—most important— within the White House. Like Murrow, he had influence, and his reporting, like Murrow's, helped nudge America toward war.

※   ※   ※   ※

Churchill recognized the importance of smooth management of information for domestic and overseas consumption. He needed to maintain morale at home and encourage interventionism in the United States, and for both those tasks he had to rely on the Ministry of Information. But during the early stages of the war, MoI was a mess—a battlefield on which intellectuals played at office politics and a bureaucracy with long but uncoordinated tentacles. Its leaders tended to serve poorly and briefly. Fed up with failure at the ministry, Churchill turned to Brendan Bracken, one of his closest aides, to take charge.

Bracken was described by politician and diarist Chips Channon as "bombastic, imaginative, and kindly." An Irishman who had risen from poverty to become a wealthy newspaper executive, Bracken had stayed with Churchill during the years in the wilderness when Churchill's warnings about Europe's perilous future were taken seriously by few. Bracken was sufficiently abrasive to put some of Churchill's other staff members on their guard. John Colville, the prime minister's private secretary, first judged Bracken to be "a cad, 'slick' and amusing, and quite likeable in his way; but rather too talkative and apt to make the most ridiculous pronouncements." An example of such pronouncements was Bracken's frequently told story of how his brother had been killed in combat, described with moving details that brought his listeners to tears. The tale was total fabrication.[64]

Among Bracken's first assignments at 10 Downing Street was to supervise the appointment of bishops, which Colville found "a little hard to stomach" because he thought the intensely political Bracken was "not the man to deal with bishops." But Colville later added a note to his journal entry about this, saying "I did not appreciate Brendan's genuine and conscientious interest in things ecclesiastical, hidden behind a mask of agnosticism," and added that Bracken had set politics aside and stated his criteria for bishops as being, "We need saints, not good administrators."[65] That was Bracken's way; after leaving a bad first impression he would surprise people and win them over with his intelligence and charm.

As far as Churchill was concerned, one of Bracken's most valuable attributes was his knowledge of American politics. He understood the popular appeal of isolationism, the influence of journalists such as Murrow, and the political maneuvers undertaken by Roosevelt. When Harry Hopkins first came to Britain in January 1941, Churchill had no idea who he was. It was Bracken who pronounced Hopkins "the most important American visitor we had ever had. He had come to tell the president what we needed and to form an opinion of the country's morale. He could influence the president more than any living man."[66]

This was the kind of knowledge that Churchill wanted to exploit at the Ministry of Information. When Bracken took over, his instructions to the ministry's American Division were straightforward: "Draw the Americans into the war." He named as new head of the division a newspaper editor who had worked as a correspondent in the United States, and he told the House of Commons that getting news to America was the most important part of his job. He lobbied American reporters such as Walter Graebner of *Life,* whom he asked to "nail any lies about Britain" when he returned home and to "tell everyone you meet what a grand nation we are."[67]

Bracken possessed detailed knowledge about the workings of the American news business as well as American politics. Knowing that Roosevelt read *The Washington Post* every morning, Bracken courted *Post* owner Eugene Meyer. He wrote to Meyer: "England will never forget what America is doing for her. And I believe that this War will not have been in vain if it ends by welding the foreign, naval, and military policies of England and America into an instrument which can stifle the rebirth of tyranny, race prejudice, and all the other beastly systems bred by Nazis and Fascists. We are having a rough time, but our people are very cheerful, and inflexible in their determination to carry this War through to a successful conclusion. Grief, destruction, and death must be our lot for many months, and perhaps years, to come. But we shall never surrender. And we are getting stronger and our people are adapting themselves to bombing and all the other hardships created by War." Meyer, who was in favor of intervention, replied: "America is profoundly impressed by the splendid defense put up by your people by air warfare and the high morale of a united people."[68]

Despite Bracken's adroitness in dealing with American journalists, Churchill worried that his friend would be unable to balance the competing interests of British politicians, military officials, and journalists. The prime minister said he was afraid that MoI "may break Brendan," but Lord Beaverbrook, the press baron who had been minister of information during World War I and was working wonders as minister of aircraft production, wrote to Bracken: "In the ordinary way it would be looked on as sarcastic or even unfriendly to offer a man congratulations on becoming

Minister of Information. In your case, this is not so. You are going to make a great success of this office. Your gifts of imagination and energy will be given a scope they have never enjoyed before. And the glory you win will be all the brighter because it shines in a dark and dismal sky."[69]

Bracken was determined to give the news media primacy among his constituencies. At his first meeting with reporters after assuming the job, he said: "I am myself a press man. I am interested in news and if I cannot get news into the papers, the sooner I depart from these premises the better for you, the better for the country, and the better for all of us." He stressed that the best way to ensure that the truth would be told was to leave that job to journalists. He promptly made more military news available and pleased reporters by throwing in tidbits from his late-night chats with Churchill. Harold Nicolson later told the House of Commons that Bracken had "convinced the press that the Ministry of Information is for their assistance and does not seek to exercise over them any form of masterdom." Bracken himself was pleased that no longer was London gossip abuzz with stories of MoI backstabbing and incompetence. With considerable satisfaction, he declared, "We are now less exciting than the British Museum."[70]

Bracken's work at MoI was driven partly by his desire to help Churchill and the war effort, and also by his genuine belief in the importance of the freest possible flow of news. "This is a people's war," he said, "and the people must be told the news about the war because without them and their spirit we cannot achieve victory." He told one member of Parliament that "the freedom of the press is as important as the freedom of parliament," and said to a reporter that constructive criticism from journalists was helpful because "complacency in wartime is a deadly sin."[71]

Finding that the news media even in friendly countries such as the United States were underrating British military efforts, Bracken made certain that troop deployments would be accompanied by a press unit to record their operations. He also had to address Churchill's concerns about the larger picture of British public opinion, particularly in terms of attitudes about the Soviet Union, which was now an ally but—as Churchill knew—not truly a friend. The prime minister instructed Bracken to have MoI "consider what action was required to counter the present tendency of the British people to forget the dangers of Communism in their enthusiasm over the resistance of Russia."[72]

Bracken was adroit at jousting with reporters. When a *New York Times* correspondent asked Bracken if the naming of a general to be the new Viceroy of India meant that India was to become a police state, Bracken quickly reeled off the names of every U.S. president who had been a general and asked the reporter if that meant America had become a police state. He dealt with long-distance complaints as well, such as a message from Harry Hopkins about "the concerted attack in the British press on two fronts: one that we won't fight and the other that our supplies are very slow. These editorials don't sit very well over here, but I presume there is some good reason for the outburst." While he tried to mollify the likes of Hopkins in Washington, Bracken also watched over the press corps in London with a mother hen's attention. He chided Murrow, who later in the war was flying on dangerous bombing runs over Germany to gather material for his broadcasts. "Your attempts to corner trouble," said Bracken, "are altogether deplorable. The value of your work cannot be overestimated and no one can take your place."[73]

Such finger-shaking aside, Bracken and Murrow were very much in tune with each other's views of the news media's rights and influence. While running MoI, Bracken operated on the principle that ensuring press freedom trumped managing press content. Murrow, who since the first days of the war had fought for better access and greater latitude in reporting, felt more comfortable in dealing with Bracken's MoI than with the ministry when it was run by officials more concerned about politics than news.

Information was flowing to the United States. What Americans would do with it remained open to question.

❋   ❋   ❋   ❋

For the Murrows, it was time to go home. Ed and Janet were rubbed raw by work and war, and CBS approved a three-month break. It was not to be leisure time, however; Ed would be traveling around the United States to promote the network and Janet would undertake her own speaking tour on behalf of Bundles for Britain. Ed sent cables to Harry Hopkins and Averill Harriman saying he hoped to see them while he was home, and he received a letter from British ambassador Lord Halifax asking to see Ed when he came to Washington. (Ed had once described Halifax as having an "elastic conscience" because of his willingness to deal with Hitler during the early months of the war.)[74]

Both Ed and Janet had mixed feelings about leaving. Janet wrote to her parents: "As the time draws nearer, I want less and less to go. It's silly, I know. I'm sure to come back, and somehow England will still be here and still be England; but I have a strange feeling that the country just can't get on without me! Everyone who loves the place and has to leave feels the same way."[75] Ed wrote to a friend in the States about suggestions that he remain in America once he returned, saying that he had chosen to return to England: "I'm not recklessly in love with this country, and some of its officials don't love me too dearly, but the fate of all of us is going to be decided over here in the next couple of years, and naturally I want to be here." He told John Winant: "Leaving this country at this time is not easy. It is, in fact, more difficult than I had expected." Ed received a note from Harold Laski in the scholar's tiny handwriting: "I hate to think of you leaving because while you are here I know that there is one person speaking to America who will put truth in the first place and not in the second. . . . I think you have done a difficult job extremely well. I think you have done honor to the tradition of America."[76]

As he made ready to depart, Ed wrote a lighthearted note to his friends at the BBC American Liaison Unit: "The purpose of this epistle, which if carried to sufficient length would reek of pusillanimous high-mindedness, is merely to say that I have occasionally cursed you and invariably enjoyed working with you. While at home, I shall be listening to my colleagues talking from

[Studio] B 4, while imagining the conversations that have preceded air time. Without disrespect to my colleagues, my imagination will be better than their broadcasts."[77]

In October, John Winant was able to secure a hard-to-come-by seat on the Atlantic Clipper from Lisbon for Janet. (Concerning this flight, Janet received a delicately phrased request from Miss H. B. Tull of the Ministry of Information: "Since every ounce of weight is budgeted for in arranging these flights, I have to ask you if you would be so good as to let me have your approximate weight fully dressed." Janet promptly responded: 135 pounds.)[78] Janet wrote to Winant to thank him for a going-away gift of orchids as well as for "your great assistance in getting me a passage. Ed hated to bother you—as did I. But it seemed the only way."[79]

Ed departed the following month by sea. The Murrows arrived in an America that was moving ever closer to war. A *Fortune* magazine poll in late summer found that only 16 percent of respondents were against "any warlike move at all," and more than 75 percent were "willing to follow President Roosevelt's foreign policy, even if it leads to war." Finally recognizing Germany's menace, 72 percent said that "Hitler will try to conquer the world." On the radio, debate continued. *Time* found that during the first ten months of 1941, interventionists aired sixty-eight programs and isolationists aired seventy-two.[80]

Roosevelt was far less coy about where he was taking America, saying in a Labor Day radio address, "I know that I speak the conscience and determination of the American people when I say that we shall do everything in our power to crush Hitler and his Nazi forces." At that point, "everything" still did not include declaring war, although one British observer noted that "the President has been quite deliberately trailing his coat all over the Atlantic for Hitler to stamp on, and Hitler has simply refused to do so."[81]

In mid-September, Hitler—however inadvertently—stamped on FDR's coat. A German U-boat and the American destroyer *Greer* exchanged volleys of torpedoes and depth charges in the North Atlantic (with no damage to either). Although there was no positive evidence that the Germans knew the nationality of the ship they were attacking, Roosevelt announced a new "shoot on sight" policy. He warned a national radio audience that Germany was intent on "domination of the Western Hemisphere by force of arms" and said that Americans must "stop being deluded by the romantic notion that the Americas can go on living happily and peacefully in a Nazi-dominated world." He added that the attack on the *Greer* "was one determined step toward creating a permanent world system based on force, on terror, and on murder."[82]

Robert E. Wood, head of America First, said that Roosevelt "has initiated an undeclared war in plain violation of the Constitution. . . . The attempt to take the American people into war, in betrayal of the most solemn promises a candidate ever made to his people, will be repudiated." Wood was wrong; that repudiation did not occur. A Gallup Poll found that 62 percent of respondents approved of the president's speech. In Britain, Churchill wrote to a friend, "As we used to sing at Sandhurst, 'Now we shan't be long!'"[83]

Although valid questions were raised then and later about whether Roosevelt had exceeded his Constitutional authority with his declaration of almost-war, his response to the *Greer* incident was just another step on a path that he had been following more and more openly since the 1940 election. By the time Murrow returned home in late November, America's formal entry into war, which he had been supporting for so long, was just weeks away.

Chapter **5**

"We Are All in the Same Boat Now"

They cheered when Ed Murrow stepped to the rostrum, and kept cheering.

More than a thousand formally dressed movers and shakers—most of whom had never before seen this slight young man, although they certainly knew his voice—rose from their seats in the Waldorf-Astoria ballroom to applaud the returning hero. Janet Murrow later told biographer Ann Sperber that her husband had seemed "stunned by the whole thing—it was so out of our whole experience; he had absolutely no idea of the effect he had had on his audience; the home office never let you know."[1]

From the White House, Franklin Roosevelt sent his words of praise: "Ed Murrow has lived in the war since its beginning. But what is more important, he has reported the news day by day and, at the same time, has kept faith with the truth-loving peoples of the world by telling the truth when he tells the news. I doubt whether in all history there has been a time when truth in the news—when comprehensive and objective news dispatches—have ever been more needed."[2]

Archibald MacLeish, America's foremost political man of letters, defined the scope of Murrow's achievement. "Over the period of your months in London," he said, "you destroyed in the minds of many men and women in this country the superstition that what is done beyond three thousand miles of water is not really done at all; the ignorant superstition that violence and lies and murder on another continent are not violence and lies and

147

murder here." He went on to describe the power of Murrow's work: "You burned the city of London in our houses and we felt the flames that burned it. You laid the dead of London at our doors and we knew the dead were our dead—were all men's dead—were mankind's dead—and ours."[3]

Turning to face the guest of honor, MacLeish told him that his assessment of events had not gone unchallenged; the isolationists had tried to counter the effects of his words from London. "There were some in this country, Murrow, who did not want the people of America to hear the things you had to say.... There are some in this country—not many but some—who do not want the American people to know what they are up against. There are some who attempt to stop the mouths of those who tell the American people what is happening in their world—who shout war-monger at those who tell them what is happening in other countries." In the end, however, Murrow had prevailed "because you told them the truth, and because you destroyed the superstition of distance and of time which makes the truth turn false, you have earned the admiration of your countrymen."[4]

When he rose to speak, Murrow was gracious and eloquent. He noted that someone who had listened to all his London broadcasts had said, "That was Murrow's contribution to the confusion of his fellow countrymen." The confusion, he said more seriously, arose partly because "we've been trying to report a new kind of war, a war that is twisting and tearing the social, political, and economic fabric of the world."

Despite the pressures generated by Britain's fight to survive, he said, freedom continued to flourish there, as was evidenced by the relatively limited—if sometimes annoying—censorship he faced. "I have often seen British censorship stupid," he said, "but seldom sinister." Although he had spent the past two years struggling to keep censorship of his work to a minimum, he now observed that "I should be unwilling to broadcast from a nation at war without any censorship at all. The responsibility for human lives would be too great. It is impossible for the layman to know on all occasions just what piece of information, even a small detail, may cause the loss of a proud ship or a company of brave men." Addressing an issue that was to loom ever larger in journalism and international affairs, he cited the role of new technology, noting that "the very speed of modern communications—with the Germans listening to everything broadcast from London—tends to slow down the release of important news."

He then proceeded to make the case, once again, that the United States needed to consider its obligation to more forcefully intervene, to protect England and to protect itself. In Britain, he said, "The flame of courage is as high and clear as it was in the days after Dunkirk, when cannon were being taken out of museums and dragged down to the beaches, when most men, save Englishmen, despaired of England's life." These Englishmen, he said, were now asking important questions: "If America comes in, will she stay in? Does she have any appetite for the greatness that is being thrust upon her? Does she realize that this world or what is left of it will be run from either Berlin or Washington?" Murrow then posed two questions of his own that America needed to answer: "Must Britain survive in order that democracy may survive? If the answer is no, we have only the devices of insulation to consider. If the answer is yes, the question is, How far and—perhaps even to a greater degree than some over here are willing to admit—how fast shall America go?"

These were political questions and Murrow did not hesitate to ask them. But underlying these political concerns was his philosophy of journalism, which he had laid out in his broadcasts and which was integral to the news product he and his colleagues delivered from London. He told the audience at the Waldorf, "In reporting this new kind of warfare we have tried to prevent our own prejudices and loyalties from coming between you and the information which it was our duty to impart. We may not always have succeeded. An individual who can entirely avoid being influenced by the atmosphere in which he works might not even be a good reporter. . . . It is no part of a reporter's function to advocate policy. The most that I can do is to indicate certain questions facing America. You must supply the answers."[5]

That was quintessential Murrow: craft the message in such a way that it carries with it a challenge to those who receive it. There was a certain disingenuousness behind his words, as there was when he closed a broadcast a year earlier with the claim that he was delivering the news "without evaluating it in terms of personal approval or disapproval." His personal opinion was very clear, and his listeners at the New York dinner were being challenged to think, decide, and act.

He may have been in white tie this night, and Kate Smith may have been waiting in the wings to entertain the crowd, but his message was little different than it had been for the past two years from London, when he pushed his listeners throughout America to make decisions about their country's direction.

※　　※　　※　　※

Before leaving England, Murrow had written to an American friend, "I hope that some of the things I've learned might be put to some use while I'm home." But he quickly found that coming to the United States from England was like traveling to another planet, and he wrote to Harold Laski that "I am bewildered and more than a little baffled, spending most of my time trying to keep my temper in check. It was a shock to see so many well-dressed, well-fed, complacent-looking people." He discovered that many Americans did not understand what was happening in Britain. He told Laski: "I have found it impossible to explain to some of your good friends why you will not leave England now. To me it is the simplest thing in the world, but they can't understand. Maybe it was a mistake for me to come."[6]

Voices of frustration were increasingly being heard in England, as well. *The Times* had recently printed a letter to the editor that read in part: "It seems strange to me that in two years of exhortation the moral argument has never been emphasized as the principal argument for American entry into the war. . . . An Englishman cannot judge. But since he cannot presume to tell America how to defend herself, nor to ask further bounty from a country which has been so bountiful, his appeal to her at the beginning of the third year of war can only be an appeal to chivalry."[7] That letter came from Cotchford Farm in Sussex, also known as Pooh Corner, and was written by A. A. Milne.

Although America had remained a bastion of indecision throughout the first years of the war, by late 1941 most of the country was in step with Roosevelt's increasingly bellicose policy. This evolution of U.S. public opinion had been gradual—far too slow to suit Murrow—but a review of polling information finds that pronounced shifts had occurred.

Before the war, as Hitler's aggressiveness had mounted, Americans were wary but inattentive. In late 1937, by which time Hitler had remilitarized the Rhineland and begun persecuting Jews, 62 percent of respondents to a *Fortune* magazine survey said they were neutral in their attitude toward Germany. After the Munich agreement of September 1938, polls found 56 percent support for boycotting German goods, but only 33 percent wanted the president to condemn Germany, and 94 percent declared themselves opposed to U.S. participation in another world war. Six weeks later, the Nazi rampage of *kristallnacht* generated more support for a boycott, taking it up to 61 percent, and after the takeover of Czechoslovakia the following spring, support reached 65 percent, but only 16 percent approved of sending U.S. troops to help Britain and France should the need arise.[8]

During the summer of 1939, 74 percent of American survey respondents said they believed war was very unlikely to break out that year. If it should happen, 84 percent said they would want Britain and France to win, while just 2 percent chose Germany, and 14 percent had no opinion. Despite this support for the democracies, only 12 percent endorsed sending U.S. forces abroad "to fight enemies of England and France."[9]

When the war began, the percentage supporting sending U.S. troops to fight alongside the British and French rose to 21 percent, but only briefly. Within two weeks, the number had fallen to 6 percent, and only 23 percent favored joining the fight even if it appeared that Britain and France seemed headed for defeat unless they received American help on the battlefield. Selling war materials to Britain, France, and Poland won approval from 63 percent during the first days of September, but the number dropped to 57 percent as it became clear that Germany's invasion of Poland could not be stopped. Although Britain and France did nothing to prevent Poland's fall, an overwhelming majority of Americans retained confidence in an eventual British-French victory: 85 percent in September and 90 percent in late October 1939.[10]

After that, Americans began backing away from Britain and France. During the "phony war" extending into spring 1940, support for America declaring war on Germany if Britain and France were losing dropped to 9 percent by April.[11] Perhaps this was a function of the same dispiriting "Chamberlain effect" that was driving Churchill to distraction. Another factor that dampened American enthusiasm for helping Britain and France was the forceful advocacy of the U.S. isolationist movement during the first stages of the war. Ten days after war was declared, Roosevelt called for a special session of Congress to repeal the Neutrality Act's arms embargo, but during the following week Americans heard nationwide radio addresses from isolationist leaders Charles Lindbergh, Senator William Borah, and Senator Arthur Vandenberg, all arguing that the United States should not in any way become involved in the European war.[12]

During summer 1940, after the fall of France, 35 percent favored helping Britain even at the risk of America being drawn into the war, while 61 percent said it was more important for the United States to keep out of the fight. By this point, Americans had seen the German army roll through Europe and the British escape from Dunkirk. Churchill had not been in power long enough to have made a substantial impression. For Murrow, American attitudes at this time were aggravating partly because they appeared inconsistent. When asked in late July if the United States should provide more food and war materials to Britain if it appeared certain that Britain would be defeated without such aid, 85 percent said yes. But when asked if the Neutrality Law should be changed so American ships could carry war supplies to England, 54 percent said no, and when asked if Britain should be allowed to purchase such supplies on credit, the answer was no by a 47-43 percent margin. These answers reflected a slight softening of isolationist opinion; when the buying on credit question had been asked in April, the answer was no by 61-31 percent. But with the presidential election drawing near, Roosevelt would not risk moving faster than the voters' opinions.[13]

Despite the small gains for interventionist sentiment, Murrow and others who understood the threat to America posed by Hitler must have found particularly irritating the response to a survey question about what America should do if Germany won: 65 percent said "try to get along with Germany" while 18 percent favored terminating trade and diplomatic relations.[14] Murrow had been talking for two years about the dangerous futility of trying to "get along with Germany," and he had to wonder now whether his words had any effect.

Poll results from autumn 1940, when the American radio audience was listening to Murrow's reports about British courage during the Blitz, had been somewhat encouraging. Polling in mid-September found the highest approval to date—76 percent—of the proposition that America should do everything possible to help Britain short of going to war. Similarly, the survey question about the relative importance of staying out of the war or helping Britain even at the risk of getting into the war, found the largest support yet for the latter course—59 percent (although this dropped to 48 percent the following month and did not climb back up until late December, helped at that time by FDR's end-of-year fireside chat). As Britain proved that it could defend itself, more Americans were agreeable to extending credit for British war purchases, sending military aircraft to the RAF, and changing the Neutrality Law so American ships could carry war supplies to England.[15]

By mid-1941, Murrow could take heart from growing commitment to help England. A Gallup survey in May asked if the United States should continue to aid Britain even at the risk of being drawn into the war, and 77 percent said yes. By a slight but consistent majority, Americans also approved using the U.S. Navy to guard convoys sailing to Britain. Another encouraging sign from Murrow's standpoint was that public opinion on such matters was starting to run ahead of official policy. While the White House and Congress proceeded cautiously, the public was stiffening its resolve to help England, although often with only a bare majority—percentages in the mid-50s.[16] Still, the trend was moving in the right direction, although still too slowly for Murrow's taste.

Americans increasingly believed that Britain was holding its own against Germany. Public opinion analyst Hadley Cantril noted the close relationship between the willingness to help Britain and the expectation of an eventual British victory. "We do not like to bet on a loser," wrote Cantril, "even if he is a friend." He also observed that although isolationism was far from extinct, it was on the wane, and by mid-1941 the interventionists had become more fervent than the isolationists. Cantril wrote that interventionism had grown stronger because "most of us were simply convinced that it was to our own self-interest to defeat the Nazis. . . . Our extensive news services and mass media of communication won our confidence and kept us so well informed that we became increasingly alert to the implications events and courses of action had for our self-interest."[17]

This latter point was a salute to the impact of Murrow's work and that of other journalists who, as MacLeish had said, had "burned the city of London in our houses" so that "we felt the flames that burned it." By early 1941, Murrow's audience was estimated at fifteen million.[18]

Even more important than the news media's coverage was the skillful leadership of Franklin Roosevelt. Although Murrow and other interventionists might fume about his deliberate pace, FDR always retained a precise sense of what was politically possible—how far and how fast the public and Congress would allow him to go. During the 1940 presidential campaign, when Roosevelt and Wendell Willkie both were minimizing the likelihood of intervention, polls reflected a substantial drop in the numbers of those who favored aid to Britain at the risk of war and those who thought that the United States would eventually go to war. After the election, when Roosevelt became more assertive about helping Britain and strengthening America's overall stance versus Hitler, he brought the public with him. Beginning in May 1941, the Gallup Poll asked, "So far as you personally are concerned, do you think President Roosevelt has gone too far in his policies of helping Britain, not far enough, or about right." Commenting on the responses to that question, Cantril cited "the almost uncanny way in which the president was able to balance public opinion around his policies." Despite the steady increase in United States aid to Britain after May 1941, said Cantril, "the proportion of people who thought the President had gone too far, about right, and not far enough remained fairly constant." ("Too far" and "not enough" each had held at about 20 percent, and "about right" at around 50 percent.)[19]

By November 1941, just a few weeks before Murrow arrived in New York, the inevitability of the United States going to war seemed to have taken hold. The dominant question was "When will we fight?" Polls found that more than 80 percent of Americans expected war with Germany and close to 70 percent anticipated war with Japan. About 70 percent said that it was more important to see Germany defeated than to stay out of war, and approximately the same number said that if America's political and military leaders thought the only way to stop Germany was to go to war, then it should be done.[20]

Murrow wished those numbers were even higher, but they were a substantial improvement over those from not long before. His greatest concern at this point, as reflected in his letters to Laski and others, was that Americans did not understand what was involved in going to war, that they saw it as a kind of theater with performances kept at a safe distance. Being bombed and left without a home, facing rationing, having family members sent off to fight with many of them not returning—these remained abstractions, the stuff of radio broadcasts, perhaps, but not real issues in their lives.

And so, when he sat down to write letters to friends after his lavish welcome home at the CBS dinner, he railed against complacency and voiced his dismay that Americans still did not understand the stakes of this war or the patriotism that was holding England together. He mailed his letters on December 6.

❋   ❋   ❋   ❋

Sunday, December 7 was a decent-enough day for a determined golfer—bright and brisk, with the temperature in the forties. Murrow and some friends drove out from downtown Washington to the Burning Tree golf club in Bethesda, Maryland. While they were playing the fourth hole, a CBS messenger came to tell Murrow about reports that the U.S. naval base at Pearl Harbor had been attacked. Murrow asked the source of the report and the messenger told him Reuters. Thinking it was just another overheated rumor, Murrow said, "Pay no attention," and the foursome kept on with their game.

But others on the course began hearing the news and Murrow decided to return to his hotel, where Janet, who had also been told about the attack, was waiting. They had been invited out to dinner that night, and Janet called to see if the gathering had been cancelled. But their hostess said, "We still have to eat; we still want you to come."[21]

Their hostess was Eleanor Roosevelt. She and the president had invited the Murrows to come for a quiet meal at which Ed could brief FDR on the state of affairs in England. As it turned out, the president remained in his study next to his bedroom while Eleanor herself served a very casual dinner—scrambled eggs, pudding, and milk. Her friends Joe and Trude Lash were there and several members of the Roosevelt family dropped by. (Trude Lash later noted that scrambled eggs was all that Eleanor, who didn't cook, ever prepared for dinner.[22]) When the Murrows made ready to leave, Eleanor said that the president wanted to see Ed, so he waited in a hallway while Janet went back to the hotel.

Four years later, shortly after the war ended, questions arose about whether the upper echelons of the Roosevelt administration had had advance knowledge of the Japanese attack. Murrow thought this was out of the question. On a CBS broadcast, he recalled his evening at the White House, saying that he had had "ample opportunity to observe at close range the bearing and expression of Mr. Stimson, Colonel Knox, and Secretary Hull. If they were *not* surprised by the news from Pearl Harbor, then that group of elderly men was putting on a performance which would have excited the admiration of any experienced actor. I cannot believe that their expressions, bearing, and conversation were designed merely to impress one correspondent who was sitting outside in the hallway. It may be that the degree of the disaster had appalled them and that they had known [it was coming] for some time. . . . But I could not believe it then and I cannot do so now. There was amazement and anger on most of the faces."[23]

While Murrow was waiting, Roosevelt aide Harry Hopkins—who lived in the White House—walked by and told Ed that he could wait more comfortably in Hopkins's bedroom down the hall. The two men talked there for a while and were joined by Commerce Secretary Jesse Jones. Shortly after midnight, FDR summoned Murrow. In the president's study was a tray with beer and sandwiches (no scrambled eggs), and FDR told Ed to help himself. Roosevelt was obviously tired—his face, thought Murrow, was the same color as his gray jacket—but, Murrow said: "I have seen certain statesmen of the world in time of crisis. Never have I seen one so calm and steady." Murrow wanted to talk about Pearl Harbor, but FDR first wanted to know about London—how the people were bearing up, how mutual friends were doing. Only then did Roosevelt ask Murrow about the day's events.

"Did this surprise you?"
"Yes, Mr. President."
"Maybe you think it didn't surprise us!"

Murrow later said, "I believed him." Roosevelt then talked about the magnitude of the losses and the lack of alertness that allowed the Japanese to approach Hawaii undetected. He pounded his fist on the table as he described the destruction of U.S. aircraft: "On the ground, by God, on the ground!"[24]

The two men were joined by Bill Donovan, who had been sent on overseas fact-finding missions by the president and would soon be named the first director of the Office of Strategic Services, predecessor of the Central Intelligence Agency. Roosevelt asked Murrow and Donovan about how U.S. public opinion would respond to the attack, and both men told the president that Americans would strongly support a declaration of war against Japan and against Germany and Italy.[25]

After about a half-hour, Murrow left. Roosevelt had made no mention of keeping their discussion off the record, and Murrow knew that he possessed more information than the public had received. But he was torn between his journalistic instincts and his respect for wartime secrecy. Furthermore, FDR was a friend who had unburdened himself on a terrible day. On his way out of the White House, Murrow stopped by the press office where Eric Sevareid was working. Sevareid knew Murrow had been with the president and asked what he had learned, but Murrow said only, "It's pretty bad," and walked away. Janet later said he had wrestled with whether to tell the story but decided not to do so until the war was over. His presence at the White House that night did, however, stir rumors in London, where several BBC staff members asked CBS correspondent Bob Trout, "Is this why he went home? Did he know this was going to happen?"[26]

Murrow did *not* know it was going to happen, but there was a reason that he was the one journalist to see the president that night. For the better part of two years a Roosevelt-Murrow partnership had existed, not in a formal sense but nevertheless with a clear common goal. Both men recognized that America's getting into the war would be enormously costly in lives and resources, but both also knew that isolationism was dangerous to the point of being suicidal. Murrow's great fear was that the United States would opt for a Chamberlain-like effort to placate Hitler, which he knew would prove as disastrous to America as it had been to Britain. Roosevelt agreed with Murrow's view about intervention and carefully undermined appeasement-inclined figures such as Joseph Kennedy. Like Murrow, FDR possessed a shrewd understanding of the power of radio, which he used so effectively in his fireside chats, and he appreciated how Murrow's broadcasts influenced public opinion.

There were no secret meetings or pacts between the journalist and the politician; they were comfortable with unspoken agreement. Also, although Murrow may have been an advocate on FDR's side, the relationship had its limits. Years before, Murrow's colleague Walter Lippmann had written speeches for Woodrow Wilson and had even helped formulate Wilson's Fourteen Points, which the president had hoped would permanently reshape European politics. More recently, journalists had been part of the Century Group, an organization of establishment figures who lobbied for increased aid to Britain. Members included *Time* publisher Henry Luce, *Louisville Courier Journal* editor Herbert Agar, and New York *Herald Tribune* editorial writers Walter Millis and Godfrey Parsons.[27] Murrow never became as close to the White House as Lippmann had been or joined any lobbying groups. He and the president just kept moving toward their shared goal with similar determination, and the Japanese attack ensured that they would reach it.

While the White House was dealing with the first reports from Pearl Harbor, Winston Churchill was at Chequers, where John Winant and Averill Harriman had joined him for dinner. They turned on the radio a moment too late to catch the beginning of the BBC's 9 PM news, and so the first items they heard were reports from the Russian and Libyan fronts. Then the announcer repeated the lead story: a Japanese air attack on Hawaii. Winant called the White House and put Churchill on the line with Roosevelt. The prime minister asked, "What's this about Japan?" and FDR replied, "It's quite true. They have attacked us at Pearl Harbor. We are all in the same boat now."[28]

Churchill later recalled that Winant and Harriman "did not wail or lament that their country was at war. They wasted no words in reproach or sorrow. In fact, one might almost have thought they had been delivered from a long pain."[29]

❋   ❋   ❋   ❋

America's entry into the war also delivered Murrow from the long pain of watching his country fail to respond with appropriate wisdom and energy to the jeopardy of its most valuable ally. He knew that now Britain would be rescued; the stream of U.S. aid would become a river and before long massive numbers of American troops would supplement the depleted British forces.

Despite the tumult of events, Ed and Janet kept to their plans for Christmas—a quiet break in Ponte Vedra Beach, Florida. While there, they pondered the future—their own as well as their country's and the world's. Immediately ahead were separate lecture tours that had been planned months before and now would feature new perspectives on America's relationship with Britain.

Murrow's friend Archibald MacLeish had a good understanding of the rapid change in American public opinion as the United States assumed responsibility for winning the war. "Down to the time when the Japanese attacked us at Pearl Harbor," he wrote, "our talk of war was talk not of affirmative purpose, but defense. Our only question was the question whether we should fight at all. The debate among us was debate upon the issue whether it was true we also were in danger—whether we too would be attacked and must prepare. That the United States should make a war affirmatively and of its own motion to accomplish some end or purpose of its own was in no one's mind." Americans' only real choice, he said, was "to fight while we still could—while we had friends to help us—or else to fight too late." Now, he said, "the American people have recaptured the current of history and they propose to move with it; they do not mean to be denied."[30]

In England, there was a sudden expansion of focus as Britons looked beyond Europe and into the Pacific, where the Japanese had attacked Hong Kong, Singapore, and other British possessions. Writing from London, Mollie Painter-Downes noted that

"Suddenly and soberly, this little island was remembering its vast and sprawling possessions of Empire. It seemed as though every person one met had a son in Singapore or a daughter in Rangoon; every post office was jammed with anxious crowds finding out about cable rates to Hong Kong, Kuala Lumpur, or Penang."

When the United States officially went to war against Germany and Italy, the news was received with little outward jubilation, wrote Painter-Downes, because it was "an event which every intelligent Briton had been quite frankly praying for ever since it became evident that, for all the fine phrases, something more than the tools was going to be necessary before there could be a possibility of finishing the job." The prevalent feeling in England was that a lengthy war lay ahead, but there was considerable optimism about long-term prospects. Painter-Downes wrote that "in spite of the sickening wallops which the democracies have taken at the beginning of this latest phase of the war, the general mood is confident." That confidence was buoyed by Churchill's trip to Washington, where he and Roosevelt publicly proclaimed the alliance of warriors that had for so long been constrained by American politics. When Churchill addressed a joint session of Congress, wrote Painter-Downes, his speech "and his warm reception were heard by millions of Britons, who sat beaming by their radios, feeling that old Winnie was doing them proud."[31]

Ed and Janet, meanwhile, pulled themselves away from the Florida beach and began their speaking tours. Over the next five weeks, Janet would make fifteen talks to a total audience of about 10,000. Her principal topic was Bundles for Britain, which had—largely through her efforts—become widely known in the United States. Soon after she had returned to the United States, she had told a New York luncheon audience, in a speech that was broadcast to England, that aid organizations were links of "good-will and friendship" between the two nations. She recounted how recipients in hospitals were reading up on the American cities from which Bundles chapters were sending clothing and other gifts.[32]

After Pearl Harbor, Janet broadened her topic to give her audiences a better understanding of the character of their British ally and to let Americans know that they should take their new tasks seriously. She noted that many in England had been slow to prepare for war even after Hitler had moved into Poland. "During the nine months before Dunkirk," she said, "the wisest of the English tore their hair and wondered whether their country would ever get under way. But since Dunkirk, everything has been on the double-quick." At last, she said, the British recognized that they were "witnessing a world revolution: the individual against a completely state-dominated system; freedom against slavery."

Echoing Ed's broadcasts, Janet described an air raid: "It's a combination of a cyclone and an earthquake, with a background of a tremendous thunder storm. It goes on endlessly. . . . Everyone's very, very scared. But even so the people will never leave their cities." She told a horrific story about a London woman who had lost her fourteen-year-old son and baby daughter in a raid and then said to her audience: "I hope that you will never have to know the horror of a night of bombing. If you have to suffer as this woman did, of course you will do it as bravely." And then she warned them again about the danger of lapsing into complacency as Britain had done during the war's first year.[33] It was a moving speech and, much like Ed's reporting, it gave Americans a sense of war as pain-filled reality rather than political abstraction.

Ed was off on his own speaking tour, covering more than 17,000 miles during the first three months of 1942. He received substantial speaking fees but said he didn't feel he should profit by telling stories about the heroism of others, and so he gave the money away, principally to an RAF fund and his alma mater, Washington State University.[34]

American news organizations were determining what adjustments they would need to make during wartime, and CBS executive Ed Klauber asked Murrow for an analysis of how the BBC operated. This gave Ed a chance to step back and evaluate the organization that he had grown so close to while in London. During his tour, Ed wrote a memo—"dictated beside the railroad tracks in the charming city of Roanoke"—that pointed out differences between the British and American broadcasting models and recommended changes that CBS might consider. He noted that the British public "has come to prefer its news straight," meaning without commentators' opinions about events. The BBC feared, said Murrow, "that one man might develop too great a personal following, making it difficult to dismiss him when his views did not coincide with those of the Corporation or the Government," a prescient observation that foreshadowed CBS's attitude toward Murrow some years later when he insisted on maintaining journalistic standards that his bosses thought were excessive. At the beginning of the war, the BBC had loosened its policy, allowing announcers to identify themselves so listeners might become acquainted with their voices in case the Germans tried to use BBC frequencies for their own purposes. Even with this exception, said Murrow, the announcers' performances were carefully monitored, and they "were instructed to read news calmly, avoiding exaltation or dismay." He added that "whenever an announcer by timing or inflection reflected his personal opinion of the news there were angry protests in the press," an inhibiting kind of censorship that Murrow was happy to have escaped.

Murrow criticized some aspects of BBC journalism. He said that BBC news was mostly "a rewrite job" based on wire service material, and he noted shortcomings in overseas coverage, stating that the BBC had "originated no broadcasts from Vienna at the time of the Anschluss, none from Munich, and very few from France, even after the outbreak of the war."

The BBC's experience provided lessons for American broadcasters. Murrow noted that British radio had delivered "technical instructions concerning civil defense, agricultural controls, and rationing" that were so lengthy and complicated that "it was impossible for the listener to understand them." Even public service broadcasts, said Murrow, needed to be well written based on an understanding of how the audience digested information delivered by radio.

For security reasons, no eyewitness accounts of in-progress air raids had been allowed, except Murrow's own. Although he had fought to be allowed to do those reports, Murrow now told CBS that such a ban "might usefully be considered here. From my own experience I am convinced that such broadcasts are difficult to do without giving information to the enemy." Murrow also noted that news organizations needed to encourage the government to maintain a steady flow of accurate information. He cited cases in which the British military had failed to correct false stories planted by the Germans, and when people eventually learned that they had been misled, even if unintentionally, their confidence in the integrity of the news media dropped.

After "having studied British broadcasting for five years," Murrow had decided that censorship caused fewer problems than did direct government involvement in managing the BBC. By accommodating officials from the Foreign Office and the Ministry of Economic Warfare, the BBC found itself taking orders from people who did not understand the realities of putting a good product on the air. Murrow's report implicitly recommended that CBS and other American news organizations work closely with the official U.S. war effort and accept a certain degree of censorship, but not surrender managerial and stylistic control to government bureaucrats.[35] Even that was a somewhat compliant position for a man who had so tenaciously battled British officialdom to get more information and win greater freedom to report. But Murrow may have thought that closeness between news media and government would be necessary because of America's naïveté about what lay ahead. He agreed with Harold Laski, who had written him several weeks after the Pearl Harbor attack that "it is a grim road we have to travel, with grim lessons to learn."

Murrow was sometimes pessimistic about the Anglo-American partnership, fearing that it had been poisoned by America's reluctance to act more promptly and forcefully. Shortly before returning to the United States he had written, "We might admit openly that America and Americans are not universally popular in Britain, and that the war aim of a great many Americans is nothing more than a Europe that won't bother them."[36] Even after Pearl Harbor, he remained concerned that Americans were not realistic in their preparations for war. During his speaking tour, he wrote to CBS president William Paley: "Some of the things I am discovering, or think I am discovering, are very disturbing. The parallels between Britain in the first year and our own position are not pleasant to contemplate."[37]

What Ed did contemplate was how he might now best serve the cause of defeating the Axis powers. Playwright and FDR speechwriter Robert E. Sherwood was setting up the Office of War Information, which would disseminate American propaganda overseas. Much of the world's radio audience spoke English, and Sherwood wanted Murrow to deliver the U.S. message. When Murrow declined, Sherwood turned to Harry Hopkins at the White House for help. Sherwood said that for broadcasts in English, which "are widely heard and understood in all countries on the [European] continent . . . we are most anxious to get Ed Murrow. His voice, his style of delivery, and his general attitude are just right. Indeed we would like to use these Ed Murrow broadcasts all over the world." Although Murrow had said he wanted to return to Britain, Sherwood told Hopkins that "it seems to me he could do far more important work here." He asked that Hopkins, and perhaps even the president, exert pressure on Murrow to remain. Hopkins tried, sending a telegram to Murrow in which he said: "It seems to me you should be related to the government and this stuff is right up your alley. I do hope you will decide to do it instead of going back to England."

But Ed remained convinced that he could best serve in London, where he could help nurture America's still-fragile relationship with Britain. He cabled Hopkins: "After much soul searching am convinced my duty is to go back to London. Believe five years training there plus opportunity to do some broadcasting for BBC makes services in common cause more valuable there than here and that's the only thing interests me. It would be personally more pleasant remain here but foreseeing troublous times ahead for Anglo-American alliance am convinced it's my duty to go back."[38]

That pretty much sums up Murrow's outlook. His longtime

goal of having America formally join the fight against Hitler had finally been reached and the Churchill-Roosevelt partnership had been publicly proclaimed and reinforced. Nevertheless, Murrow did not feel that he could walk away from his friends in Britain. Their story still needed to be told, and he expected that before long American resolve would require bolstering. London was the best place for him to help do all that.

※　　※　　※　　※

By late April, Murrow was once again broadcasting from London. He found that problems persisted in the partnership between the allies, with Britons growing impatient as the United States organized itself for war. In a broadcast that summer, Murrow said: "Some effort to explain America to the British people might smooth the path of Anglo-American relations now and in the future. But it is so far no part of our government policy to do so. Everyone agrees that there has never been a time when the British have been more anxious and willing to learn about American affairs and institutions, but we do nothing about it. You would find no outspoken anti-American sentiments over here. But the British themselves sat surrounded by their oceans, filled with pride and ignorance, for too long not to resent it when another country adopts the same attitude."[39]

At the end of August Murrow marked the war's third anniversary, noting that "three years is long enough for schoolboys to grow up and become soldiers but not long enough to permit you to forget the friends who have died." He urged his listeners to recognize that the United States retained its privileged status in terms of enjoying levels of safety and comfort that were vague memories for those in Europe. "We are the only people fighting this war," he said, "with plenty of food, clothing, and shelter, with an undamaged productive system that can work in the light. We aren't tired, and Europe is—all of it. We lack the incentive of the imminence of immediate danger." A few months later, he observed that "on occasion we have done less than our allies expected. But we have done more than our enemies believed possible. We have not fought and suffered as the Russians, nor have we sacrificed as the British, but we have brought hope and confidence to a world that was waiting."[40]

By the end of 1942, the American presence in Britain was large and growing, soon to reach 1,500,000 servicemen. U.S. Ambassador John Winant delivered a series of talks on the BBC, "Let's Get Acquainted," to prepare Britons for their visitors.[41] The Americans also needed preparation, so the U.S. War Department issued a pamphlet of "Instructions for American Servicemen in Britain," which told U.S. soldiers that "the British are tough. Don't be misled by the British tendency to be soft-spoken and polite. . . . You won't be able to tell the British much about 'taking it.' They are not particularly interested in taking it any more. They are far more interested in getting together in solid friendship with us, so that we can all start dishing it out to Hitler." The Americans were also reminded that the British did not "need to be told that their armies lost the first couple of rounds in the present war. . . . Use your head before you sound off, and remember how long the British alone held Hitler off without any help from anyone." On a more personal level, the soldiers were urged to remember that "you are coming to Britain from a country where your home is still safe, food is still plentiful, and lights are still burning. So it is doubly important for you to remember that the British soldiers and civilians have been living under tremendous strain. It is always impolite to criticize your hosts. It is militarily stupid to insult your allies."[42]

For their part, Britons were curious about their guests and eager to emulate some aspects of their behavior. "A year ago," reported Murrow, "you seldom saw an English girl chewing gum; now if you visit a town where American troops are stationed, the girls seem to be chewing as though trying to make up for lost years. The first year of global war brought the Americans to Britain, and the place will never be the same again."[43]

Although Murrow sometimes offered these light sketches as part of his broadcasts, most of his reporting concentrated on the dark reality of the war. He was one of the first journalists to take note of what was happening to Europe's Jews, reporting in December 1942 that "millions of human beings, most of them Jews, are being gathered up with ruthless efficiency and murdered. . . . The phrase 'concentration camps' is obsolete; it is now possible to speak only of extermination camps." Murrow also began to travel from London to see the war for himself. To meet U.S. soldiers on their way into combat, he went home to America and then came back across the Atlantic on the *Queen Elizabeth*, which was being used as a troopship. He went to North Africa where he described the sights of the front lines, such as walking along a stream where "a German soldier sits smiling against the bank. He is covered with dust and he is dead. On the rising ground beyond, a young British lieutenant lies with his head on his arm as though shielding himself from the wind. He is dead, too."[44]

On several occasions, he flew on bombing missions over Germany, admitting that when his plane was caught in German searchlights "I was very frightened." As he looked down on Berlin while heavy bombs and packets of incendiaries were being dropped, he saw that "the white fires had turned red. They were beginning to merge and spread, just like butter does on a hot plate." He said that "Berlin was a kind of orchestrated hell, a terrible symphony of light and flame. . . . Men die in the sky while others are roasted alive in their cellars. . . . This is a calculated, remorseless campaign of destruction." On the night of this flight, two journalists who were in other planes did not make it back; one was killed and the other parachuted and was captured.[45]

In the summer and fall of 1944, as Allied armies fought their way across Europe, the Germans gave England a vicious reminder of what life had been like during the Blitz. First came the V-1 flying bombs. Beginning in June, on average seventy-three of them hit London every twenty-four hours, but as many as 200 per day arrived when the weather was bad enough to hinder the pilots and anti-aircraft batteries that tried to shoot them down. In the London area, the V-1s killed more than 5,000 and seriously injured 15,000 more.[46]

As this barrage tapered off, Londoners thought that perhaps the worst was now truly over. Herbert Morrison, the home secretary and minister of home security, wrote a tribute to London that said in part: "To Hitler, London is and always has been a strong-point of immense significance in the fighting line against him. The enemy has stated time and again that the object of his flying bomb and other secret weapons is to break our will to win. That is what he has been trying to do—to break the spirit of London, to make London squeal to such a pitch that the Government would be forced to call off the war. . . . The day has come when London can openly rejoice in the great part she has played in the overthrow of Nazism by the sturdiness of her resistance, first in 1940 and now in the last battles of the war."[47]

Morrison's tribute appeared in *The Times* September 7. The next day, the first V-2 hit London.

The V-1s were bad enough, but they were basically just another form of aircraft and conventional countermeasures could be taken against them. The V-2s were supersonic missiles. They were launched from a German base in The Netherlands, reached London in four minutes, and were visible for only about four seconds in the final stage of their descent. Scrambling fighters and firing antiaircraft batteries were not options; only the missiles' own imperfect technology could do them in. They caused substantial damage and battered the morale of already exhausted Britons, who were told little about the V-2 because of censorship rules meant to deprive the Germans of information about the weapon's effectiveness.

Their effectiveness was frightening. One V-2 that landed in the Islington section of London cleared an area about 200 yards square, demolished fifty houses, and left 200 families homeless. By the time the last one struck in late March 1945, 517 had hit in the London area, killing 2,500 persons and seriously injuring almost 6,000 more.[48] During the attacks Murrow reported that "these are days when a vivid imagination is a definite liability. There is nothing pleasant in contemplating the possibility, however remote, that a ton of high explosive may come through the roof with absolutely no warning of any kind." Looking ahead, he warned that missile warfare meant "that within a few years present methods of aerial bombardment will be as obsolete as the Gatling gun."[49]

Despite these new terrors, the war was clearly moving toward conclusion. In late November, Murrow told his listeners: "The blackout is gradually lifting. And when I leave this studio tonight, I shall walk up a street in which there is light—not much, but more than there has been for five-and-a-half years." On this street, said Murrow, was a synagogue, with a placard that had been hanging through all the bombing and said, "Blessed is he whose conscience hath not condemned him and who is not fallen from his hope in the Lord." This was Hallam Street, where the Murrows lived, and each barely glowing street lamp, said Murrow, would be "like a cathedral candle for those whose faith was greatest when the nights were darkest."[50]

❋　　❋　　❋　　❋

That winter, which was to be the last of the war, was the coldest in fifty years, so cold that it brought London's rebuilding efforts to a near standstill while everything from milk bottles to water mains froze and burst. Despite knowing that the war was painfully but certainly nearing its end, Londoners could not shake their exhaustion. Even without the constant physical danger of air raids, their nerves and lives were frayed. Food rationing was just one irritant. Imagine how you'd feel if the finest delicacy you could find was Lingford's Banana Flavoured Barley Pudding.[51]

With spring came the crumbling of the Third Reich. By April, American forces were pushing through Germany, and Murrow was with them. He reported about the military advances and the devastation of German cities, but his most famous broadcast from this time was the one he prefaced with, "I propose to tell you of Buchenwald."

He entered the camp with the liberating troops from General George Patton's Third Army. All the Americans were unprepared for what they encountered. As Murrow walked into one of the barracks, "men crowded around, tried to lift me to their shoulders. They were too weak. Many of them could not get out of bed. I was told that this building had once stabled eighty horses. There were 1,200 men in it, five to a bunk. The stink was beyond all description." He told of the children, silent and so skinny that "I could see their ribs through their thin shirts." In a courtyard "there were two rows of bodies stacked up like cordwood. They were thin and very white. . . . I tried to count them as best I could and arrived at the conclusion that all that was mortal of more than 500 men and boys lay there in two neat piles. . . . Murder had been done at Buchenwald."

Murrow went on: "I pray you to believe what I have said about Buchenwald. I have reported what I saw and heard, but only part of it. For most of it I have no words. . . . If I've offended you by this rather mild account of Buchenwald, I'm not in the least sorry."[52]

To give himself some emotional distance from what he'd seen, Murrow delayed his broadcast for several days, until he'd returned to London. The understated power of his description shook awake some who even at this late date could not or would not believe that such horrors had occurred. The BBC and a number of newspapers carried Murrow's report, thinking that their audience would believe him and not think this was propaganda, like the invented "atrocity stories" that had been common during World War I.[53]

Three weeks later—May 8, 1945—was VE day, the end of the war in Europe. Murrow described the celebration and reminded his listeners that "the price of victory has been high." Europe was in shambles, he told America, and "unknown millions have lost everything—home, families, clothes, even their very countries." Although victory was in hand, Europe was still looking to the United States to lead it into the future.

❋　　❋　　❋　　❋

On the day Murrow was at Buchenwald, President Franklin Delano Roosevelt died. The two men had been friends and firm allies in their determination to lead America into a war they both considered necessary for national survival. Eulogizing the American president in the House of Commons, Winston Churchill said, "For us, it remains only to say that in Franklin Roosevelt there died the greatest American friend we have ever known, and the greatest champion of freedom who has ever brought help and comfort from the new world to the old."[54]

Twenty years later, not long after he had watched Churchill's funeral on television, Ed Murrow died of cancer at age fifty-seven. In the years following the war, he had moved from radio to television, where he showed what the new medium could accomplish if wisely used. He continues to be regarded as one of America's greatest journalists.

He may be best known for his television documentaries and his confrontation with Senator Joseph McCarthy, but his most important achievement was his radio work from 1939 through 1941, when he awakened America and helped steel its resolve. While some believed that appeasement and isolation could buy peace, Murrow never had any doubts about the evil of Adolf Hitler, and in concert with Roosevelt and Churchill he did his best to ensure that wishful thinking would not obscure reality.

His commitment to this cause transcended journalism, which makes his story more interesting and his role more complex. Although he said on the air that he was presenting fact and not opinion, his own beliefs were never far below the surface of his reporting and they shaped the tone and heightened the impact of his broadcasts. Furthermore, although he was proud to be an American citizen, he actively assisted the British government in its efforts to pull his country into the war, advising British propagandists and even acting as a go-between for a British intelligence operation.

Was that ethical? "Objectivity" and "detachment" have been carved in stone as standards for journalists, but Murrow believed that such ideals should not be allowed to impede his ability to deliver the core truth that lay beneath the surface of the news. That truth was grounded in his belief that his country—his fellow citizens who listened to him every night—had an obligation to stand up to a horrible evil and stop it from sweeping across the world.

He thought that in extraordinary times, professional responsibility might need to be redefined. He had a clear agenda, which he relentlessly pursued. As a matter of conventional journalistic ethics, Murrow's choices might be challenged, but history has justified his actions: he was right about Hitler's menace, right about Churchill's and Roosevelt's determination to fight, and right about the need for Americans to come to Britain's rescue and join the fight against the Axis powers.

America's global role continues to be debated within the United States and throughout the world. The propriety of armed intervention is likewise still debated while the world watches evil that may not be as far reaching as was Nazi Germany's aggression but has nonetheless proved lethal to millions in central Africa, the Balkans, and elsewhere. Sometimes the powerful must act, and to ensure that they do journalists should never hesitate to jab the world's conscience and show why timely, forceful measures are essential.

Ed Murrow knew that war is always terrible but sometimes necessary. That knowledge shaped his efforts to help take America into war. He did not just report. He led.

Acknowledgments

Many people were generous with their time and expertise as they assisted me with research for this book:

At Mount Holyoke College, home of the Edward R. and Janet Brewster Murrow Papers, Patricia Albright and Jennifer Gunter King.

At the Franklin D. Roosevelt Library, Bob Clark.

At Chatham House—the Royal Institute of International Affairs—Mary Bone.

At the BBC Written Archives in Reading, England, Erin O'Neill.

At Marquette University, the staff of the Raynor Library; Provost Madeline Wake, who provided a grant to fund research travel; graduate students Chris Carlson, Matt Ruud, Kayvon Safavi, and Angela Speed, whose research projects turned up much useful material.

Others who supplied aid and counsel: Suzanne Huffman, Jim Leutze, Adam Nicolson, John Sparks, John Winant, and Rivington Winant.

Special thanks to Casey Murrow.

My agent, Robbie Anna Hare, again was a superb navigator amidst the shoals of the publishing world. Her persistence and devotion to her writers are unsurpassed.

Don McKeon at Potomac Books quickly embraced this book

and has been a pleasure to work with, as has production editor Marla Traweek.

As always, Christine Wicker sustained me, in writing and in life.

Notes

The following abbreviations are used throughout the notes section:

BBC: BBC Written Archives Centre (Caversham Park, Reading).

Chatham House: Royal Institute of International Affairs (London).

FDR Library: Franklin D. Roosevelt Library (Hyde Park, N.Y.).

MHC: Edward R. and Janet Brewster Murrow Papers, Mount Holyoke College, Archives and Special Collections (South Hadley, Mass.).

Prologue

1. Winston S. Churchill, *Memoirs of the Second World War* (Boston: Houghton Mifflin, 1959), 163.

2. Edward R. Murrow, *This Is London* (New York: Simon and Schuster, 1941), 7–8.

3. Murrow, *This Is London*, 10.

4. Joseph E. Persico, *Edward R. Murrow: An American Original* (New York: McGraw-Hill, 1988), 122.

5. Alexander Kendrick, *Prime Time: The Life of Edward R. Murrow* (Boston: Little, Brown, 1969), 234.

6. Susan J. Douglas, *Listening In: Radio and the American Imagination* (New York: Times Books, 1999), 175.

7. Persico, *Edward R. Murrow*, 137.

8. Eric Sevareid, *Not So Wild a Dream* (New York: Atheneum, 1976), 176–77.

9. Kendrick, *Prime Time*, 177.

10. Kendrick, *Prime Time*, 176.

11. Churchill, *Memoirs of the Second World War*, 163.

Chapter One

1. Paul W. White, *News on the Air* (New York: Harcourt Brace, 1947), 31.

2. Kendrick, *Prime Time*, 178.

3. David Holbrook Culbert, *News for Everyman* (Westport, Conn.: Greenwood, 1976), 113–14.

4. A. M. Sperber, *Murrow: His Life and Times* (New York: Freundlich Books, 1986), 142, 145.

5. Murrow, *This Is London*, 11, 13.

6. Paul W. White, "Covering a War for Radio," *Annals of the American Academy of Political and Social Science*, 213 (January 1941): 85.

7. White, "Covering a War for Radio," 91.

8. White, "Covering a War for Radio," 90.

9. Kendrick, *Prime Time*, 234.

10. Culbert, *News for Everyman*, 84.

11. Philip Seib, *Rush Hour: Talk Radio, Politics, and the Rise of Rush Limbaugh* (Fort Worth, Texas: Summit Group, 1993), 146–47.

12. Seib, *Rush Hour*, 149–51.

13. Kendrick, *Prime Time*, 184.

14. White, "Covering a War for Radio," 86.

15. White, "Covering a War for Radio," 90.

16. Murrow, *This Is London*, 18.

17. Anne De Courcy, *1939: The Last Season* (London: Phoenix, 2003), 246–47.

18. Kenneth D. Yeilding and Paul H. Carlson, eds., *Ah That Voice: The Fireside Chats of Franklin Delano Roosevelt* (Odessa, Texas: John Ben Shepperd, Jr. Library of Presidents, 1974), 117–19.

19. *Time*, September 11, 1939, 14.

20. *Time*, September 25, 1939, 12.

21. "Editorials Back President's Plea," *New York Times*, September 22, 1939, 19.

22. "Thomas Sees U.S. Being Led to War," *New York Times*, September 13, 1939, 8.

23. De Courcy, *1939*, 231.

24. De Courcy, *1939*, xiii, 181, 238, 244.

25. De Courcy, *1939*, x.

26. Murrow, *This Is London*, 19, 146.

27. Harold N. Graves, Jr., "Propaganda by Short Wave: London Calling America," *Public Opinion Quarterly*, 5, no. 1, 45.

28. Murrow, *This Is London*, 31–33.

29. Sperber, *Murrow*, 138.

30. Murrow, *This Is London*, 30.

31. Robert E. Herzstein, *Henry R. Luce* (New York: Scribners, 1994), 127.

32. Kendrick, *Prime Time*, 232.

33. Murrow, *This Is London*, 38.

34. Charles Merz, ed., *Days of Decision: Wartime Editorials from The New York Times* (Garden City, N.Y.: Doubleday, Doran, 1941), 17.

35. William R. Rock, *Chamberlain and Roosevelt: British Foreign Policy and the United States, 1937–1940* (Columbus, Ohio: Ohio State University Press, 1988), 255.

36. Murrow, *This Is London*, 70.

37. BBC, R 61/3/2.

38. Nicholas John Cull, *Selling War* (New York: Oxford University Press, 1995), 45.

39. BBC, "Censorship and American Liaison," R 61/3/1.

40. BBC, R 61/3/2.

41. Sperber, *Murrow*, 158–59.

42. BBC, R 61/3/1, R 61/3/2.

43. Cull, *Selling War*, 24–25.

44. BBC, Talks, Murrow, Edward, file 1, R CONT1.

45. Churchill, *Memoirs of the Second World War*, 174.

46. Philip Ziegler, *London at War 1939–1945* (London: Pimlico, 2002), 58.

47. Murrow, *This Is London*, 46.

48. David Reynolds, *From Munich to Pearl Harbor* (Chicago: Ivan R. Dee, 2001), 92.

49. Gerald Nye, "Yes, Says Nye," *New York Times*, January 14, 1940, SM 1.

50. A. Scott Berg, *Lindbergh* (New York: Berkley Books, 1999), 413, 415.

51. *Time*, September 25, 1939, 14.

52. Berg, *Lindbergh*, 402, 425.

53. Kendrick, *Prime Time*, 180, 236.

54. *Time*, September 18, 1939, 30.

55. Deborah E. Lipstadt, *Beyond Belief: The American Press and the Coming of the Holocaust* (New York: Free Press, 1986), 143.

56. *Time*, March 4, 1940, 14.

57. Vincent Sheean, *Between the Thunder and the Sun* (New York: Random House, 1943), 274.

58. Rock, *Chamberlain and Roosevelt*, 261.

59. Culbert, *News for Everyman*, 115.

60. Cull, *Selling War*, 109.

61. Culbert, *News for Everyman*, 138–39.

62. Sheean, *Between the Thunder and the Sun*, 269, 276.

63. Edward Bliss, Jr., ed., *In Search of Light: The Broadcasts of Edward R. Murrow*, New York: Knopf, 1967), 24.

64. John Lukacs, *Five Days in London, May 1940* (New Haven, Conn.: Yale University Press, 1999), 185.

65. Churchill, *Memoirs of the Second World War*, 272.

66. Lukacs, *Five Days in London*, 191.

67. Murrow, *This Is London*, 118, 120–21.

68. David M. Kennedy, *Freedom from Fear* (New York: Oxford University Press, 1999), 442.

69. Richard J. Whalen, *The Founding Father: The Story of Joseph P. Kennedy* (New York: New American Library, 1964), 216.

70. Whalen, *The Founding Father*, 246.

71. Kendrick, *Prime Time*, 194.

72. Robert Dallek, *Franklin D. Roosevelt and American Foreign Policy, 1932–1945* (New York: Oxford University Press, 1979), 207.

73. Whalen, *The Founding Father*, 276.

74. Whalen, *The Founding Father*, 285.

75. Rock, *Chamberlain and Roosevelt*, 276.

76. Whalen, *The Founding Father*, 292, 297, 303.

77. Kendrick, *Prime Time*, 195.

78. Sperber, *Murrow*, 151.

79. Doris Kearns Goodwin, *No Ordinary Time* (New York: Simon and Schuster, 1994), 212.

80. Whalen, *The Founding Father*, 300.

81. Whalen, *The Founding Father*, 287.

82. Murrow, *This Is London*, 71–72.

83. Murrow, *This Is London*, 107.

84. Murrow, *This Is London*, 101–102, 110, 122.

85. Murrow, *This Is London*, 108.

86. Harold N. Graves, Jr., "Propaganda by Short Wave: London Calling America," 38, 45, 47.

87. Murrow, *This Is London*, 76.

88. White, "Covering a War for Radio," 92.

89. Cull, *Selling War*, 85.

90. Harold N. Graves, Jr., "European Radio and the War," *Annals of the American Academy of Political and Social Science*, 213 (January 1941): 79.

91. Sperber, *Murrow*, 144, 149, 150.

92. Kendrick, *Prime Time*, 199.

93. BBC, R 61/3/2.

94. Murrow, *This Is London*, 75.

95. Charles J. Rolo, *Radio Goes to War* (New York: G. P. Putnam's Sons, 1942), 70, 75.

96. Rolo, *Radio Goes to War*, 76.

97. Graves, "European Radio and the War," 80.

98. Harold N. Graves, Jr., "Propaganda by Short Wave: Berlin Calling America," *The Public Opinion Quarterly*, 4, no. 4 (December 1940): 601, 602, 605, 606.

99. Rolo, *Radio Goes to War*, 112.

100. Graves, "Propaganda by Short Wave: Berlin Calling," 601, 606.

101. Chatham House, Ronald Tree speech, Royal Institute of International Affairs, April 4, 1940.

102. Graves, "Propaganda by Short Wave: Berlin Calling," 607, 610.

103. Rolo, *Radio Goes to War*, 120.

104. Graves, "Propaganda by Short Wave: Berlin Calling," 611, 612.

105. Rolo, *Radio Goes to War*, 121.

106. Murrow, *This Is London*, 74.

107. Sperber, *Murrow*, 147.

108. Sperber, *Murrow*, 143.

109. White, "Covering a War for Radio," 91.

110. Sperber, *Murrow*, 160.

111. Warren F. Kimball, *Forged in War* (New York: William Morrow, 1997), 44.

112. Sumner Welles, *The Time for Decision* (New York: Harper and Brothers, 1944), 134.

113. Jon Meacham, *Franklin and Winston* (New York: Random House, 2003), 48.

114. Meacham, *Franklin and Winston*, 49.

115. Rock, *Chamberlain and Roosevelt*, 267.

116. Meacham, *Franklin and Winston*, 52.

117. David Cannadine, ed., *Blood, Toil, Tears and Sweat: The Speeches of Winston Churchill* (Boston: Houghton Mifflin, 1989), 165.

118. Murrow, *This Is London*, 125.

119. Rock, *Chamberlain and Roosevelt*, 256.

120. Murrow, *This Is London*,130–31; MHC ERM letter to Alfred Cohn, June 29, 1940.

121. R. Franklin Smith, *Edward R. Murrow: The War Years* (Kalamazoo, Mich: New Issues Press, 1978), 118, 110.

122. MHC, JBM diary, July 14, 1940.

123. Smith, *Murrow: The War Years*, 118.

124. Murrow, *This Is London*,134–35.

125. MHC, ERM letter to John Marshall, June 4, 1940; ERM letter to Charles Siepmann, May 6, 1940.

126. Chatham House, RIIA/8/472 (November 23, 1937).

127. *Time*, July 1, 1940, 18.

128. Churchill, *Memoirs of the Second World War*, 335.

129. De Courcy, *1939*, 206; Royal Air Force, www.raf.mod.uk/history.

130. Murrow, *This Is London*, 153.
131. Murrow, *This Is London*, 150.

Chapter Two

1. MHC, JBM to families, July 6, July 9, and July 29, 1937; diary April 20, 1940.

2. MHC, JBM to families, July 29 and November 2, 1937, June (n.d.) 1939.

3. MHC, ERM to JBM, summer (n.d.) and August 6, 1937.

4. MHC, Janet Murrow to families, February 15, 1938, April 21, 1939, and receipt dated October 21, 1941.

5. MHC, JBM to families, November 27, 1939 and February 21, 1940; ERM to Metropolitan Police, July 16, 1940.

6. Sperber, *Murrow*, 154; MHC, JBM diary, September 4, 1939; JBM letter to family, September 8, 1939.

7. MHC, JBM to families, May 13, May 17, and August 29, 1940.

8. MHC, JBM letter to family, September 28, 1939; JBM diary, September 5, 1939.

9. MHC, JBM letters, December 20, 1939 and August 8, 1940.

10. Kendrick, *Prime Time*, 230; "19 Bombed Hospitals in London 'Adopted' by Bundles for Britain," *New York Times*, February 21, 1941, 5; "Clothing Needs of British Listed," *New York Times*, August 31, 1941, 15..

11. MHC, JBM letter, December 20, 1939; JBM diary, March 6, 1940.

12. Mollie Painter-Downes, *London War Notes 1939–1945* (New York: Farrar, Straus and Giroux, 1971), 60.

13. Kendrick, *Prime Time*, 216.

14. Raymond A. Schroth, *The American Journey of Eric Sevareid* (South Royalton, Vt.: Steerforth Press, 1995), 163.

15. Ernie Pyle, "Ed Murrow," *Washington Daily News*, March 31, 1941.

16. MHC, ERM letters, July 3, 1940 and September 15, 1941.

17. MHC, JBM letter to family, July 3, 1939.

18. Kendrick, *Prime Time*, 227.

19. MHC, JBM letters to family, June 3, 1940, February 21, 1940; Persico, *Edward R. Murrow*, 148; Cull, *Selling War*, 45.

20. MHC, ERM letter to Louis Gimbel, June 27, 1940.

21. MHC, JBM letters to Mrs. Charles Brewster, March 1 and April 18, 1941.

22. Kendrick, *Prime Time*, 231; Sperber, *Murrow*, 185; Ronald Tree, *When the Moon Was High* (London: Macmillan, 1975), 189.

23. Norman Rose, *The Cliveden Set* (London: Jonathan Cape, 2000), 11–13; De Courcy, *1939*, 130.

24. De Courcy, *1939*, 131.

25. Christopher Sykes, *Nancy: The Life of Lady Astor* (London: Collins, 1972), 381.

26. Rose, *The Cliveden Set*, 174; Sykes, *Nancy*, 366.

27. Sykes, *Nancy*, 367, 373; Rose, *The Cliveden Set*, 178.

28. Sykes, *Nancy*, 369, 372; Rose, *The Cliveden Set*, 194, 180; Harold Nicolson, *Diaries and Letters 1930–1939* (New York: Atheneum, 1966), 361, 366.

29. Sykes, *Nancy*, 379, 403; Rose, *The Cliveden Set*, 180, 183; Michael Beschloss, *Kennedy and Roosevelt* (New York: Norton, 1980), 177; Telford Taylor, *Munich: The Price of Peace* (Garden City, N.Y.: Doubleday, 1979), 763.

30. Rose, *The Cliveden Set*, 192.

31. Robert Rhodes James, *"Chips": The Diaries of Sir Henry Channon* (London: Phoenix, 1996), 154; J. R. M. Butler, *Lord Lothian* (London: Macmillan, 1960), 250; Sykes, *Nancy*, 401.

32. Sykes, *Nancy*, 389.

33. Rose, *The Cliveden Set*, 204.

34. Persico, *Edward R. Murrow*, 151.

35. Persico, *Edward R. Murrow*, 148.

36. Tree, *When the Moon Was High*, 130.

37. Tree, *When the Moon Was High*, 74.

38. Tree, *When the Moon Was High*, 103.

39. Rock, *Chamberlain and Roosevelt*, 256.

40. Tree, *When the Moon Was High*, 188–89.

41. Rock, *Chamberlain and Roosevelt*, 261.

42. Chatham House, Ronald Tree speech, April 4, 1940.

43. "Senate Body Asks for Propaganda Investigation," *New York Times*, March 26, 1940, 3.

44. Tree, *When the Moon Was High*, 154, 106; Cedric Larson, "The British Ministry of Information," *Public Opinion Quarterly*, 5, no. 3 (Autumn 1941): 430.

45. John Colville, *The Fringes of Power* (New York: W. W. Norton, 1986), 733.

46. Martin Gilbert, *Churchill* (New York: Henry Holt, 1991), 613.

47. Kendrick, *Prime Time*, 262.

48. Persico, *Edward R. Murrow*, 206.

49. Tree, *When the Moon Was High*, 157–58.

50. Tree, *When the Moon Was High*, 166, 163.

51. Butler, *Lord Lothian*, 292–93.

52. Butler, *Lord Lothian*, 298.

53. Tree, *When the Moon Was High*, 163; John Colville, *The Fringes of Power: 10 Downing Street Diaries 1939–1955* (New York: Norton, 1985), 472.

54. Sheean, *Between the Thunder and the Sun*, 214.

55. BBC, R 61/5.

56. Sheean, *Between the Thunder and the Sun*, 217.

57. Quentin Reynolds, *London Diary* (New York: Random House, 1941), 66; Quentin Reynolds, *The Wounded Don't Cry* (New York: Dutton, 1941), 252.

58. Reynolds, *London Diary*, 164–65, 302.

59. Sevareid, *Not So Wild a Dream*, 178; Sperber, *Murrow*, 172.

60. Cull, *Selling War*, 85, 87; Kendrick, *Prime Time*, 214.

61. Rolo, *Radio Goes to War*, 184, 189.

62. Cull, *Selling War*, 162; Sperber, *Murrow*, 190; Asa Briggs, *The War of Words* (London: Oxford University Press, 1970), 253.

63. Frances Stonor Saunders, *The Cultural Cold War* (New York: New Press, 1999), 135.

64. Chatham House, Minutes of the RIIA Council, April 19, 1939; Olive Renier and Vladimir Rubinstein, *Assigned To Listen* (London: BBC External Services, 1986), 16, 19.

65. Sperber, *Murrow*, 185; Kendrick, *Prime Time*, 231.

66. H. Montgomery Hyde, *Room 3603* (New York: Farrar, Straus, 1962), 35.

67. Tree, *When the Moon Was High*, 126–27; James Leutze (ed.), *The London Diary of General Raymond E. Lee 1940–1941* (Boston: Little, Brown, 1971), 27.

68. Robert H. Jackson, *That Man* (New York: Oxford University Press, 2003), 99–100.

69. Churchill, *Memoirs of the Second World War*, 385.

70. Ziegler, *London at War*, 105.

71. Murrow, *This Is London*, 152–53.

Chapter Three

1. *Front Line 1940–41: The Official Story of the Civil Defense of Britain* (London: His Majesty's Stationery Office, 1942), 12. Other reports have somewhat different figures.

2. Ziegler, *London at War*, 4.

3. John Ray, *The Night Blitz* (London: Arms and Armour, 1996), 264.

4. Sheean, *Between the Thunder and the Sun*, 225.

5. Sevareid, *Not So Wild a Dream*, 172.

6. Kendrick, *Prime Time*, 175.

7. Sheean, *Between the Thunder and the Sun*, 241.

8. "Great Britain: Never Did, Never Shall," *Time*, September 9, 1940, 29.

9. Ziegler, *London at War*, 126, 154.

10. Murrow, *This Is London*, 158, 161, 163.

11. Murrow, *This Is London*, 163.

12. Murrow, *This Is London*, 167, 170, 172, 173, 178.

13. Murrow, *This Is London*, 180, 182.

14. "British Say Court Won't Quit London," *New York Times*, September 14, 1940, 3.

15. Stanley Cloud and Lynne Olson, *The Murrow Boys* (Boston: Houghton Mifflin, 1996), 90, 97.

16. Ziegler, *London at War*, 144, 151.

17. William L. Shirer, *The Rise and Fall of the Third Reich* (New York: Simon and Schuster, 1960), 774.

18. Kendrick, *Prime Time*, 175, 207.

19. Sheean, *Between the Thunder and the Sun*, 212.

20. Sevareid, *Not So Wild a Dream*, 170; Kendrick, *Prime Time*, 206.

21. Sevareid, *Not So Wild a Dream*, 169, 171.

22. Sperber, *Murrow*, 171, 176.

23. Sheean, *Between the Thunder and the Sun*, 217; Kendrick, *Prime Time*, 189.

24. Persico, *Edward R. Murrow*, 145.

25. Murrow, *This Is London*, 214–16.

26. Sevareid, *Not So Wild a Dream*, 178.

27. Persico, *Edward R. Murrow*, 171; Bob Edwards, *Edward R. Murrow and the Birth of Broadcast Journalism* (Hoboken, N.J.: John Wiley, 2004), 52.

28. Sevareid, *Not So Wild a Dream*, 167.

29. Sperber, *Murrow*, 164, 173.

30. BBC, R 61/3/2.

31. BBC, R 61/3/2.

32. BBC, R 61/3/2.

33. Murrow, *This Is London*, 211.

34. Ernie Pyle, *Ernie Pyle in England* (New York: Robert M. McBride, 1941), 95.

35. Ziegler, *London at War*, 124, 169; J. B. Priestley, *Britain Speaks* (New York: Harper and Bros., 1940), 248.

36. Ziegler, *London at War*, 164.

37. Murrow, *This Is London*, 183.

38. Pyle, *Ernie Pyle in England*, 27, 33.

39. Pyle, *Ernie Pyle in England*, 48-–49.

40. Pyle, *Ernie Pyle in England*, 126, 225, 226.

41. Painter-Downes, *London War Notes*, 98.

42. Priestley, *Britain Speaks*, 11.

43. Priestley, *Britain Speaks*, 216.

44. Priestley, *Britain Speaks*, 13.

45. Priestley, *Britain Speaks*, 147, 142.

46. Priestley, *Britain Speaks*, 213, 218, 226.

47. Ernestine Carter, ed., *Bloody but Unbowed* (New York: Scribner's, 1941), iii.

48. BBC, RCONT1 Talks, Murrow, Edward, file 1.

49. Cull, *Selling War*, 138.

50. Reynolds, *From Munich to Pearl Harbor*, 96.

51. Quentin Reynolds, *Britain Can Take It* (New York: Dutton, 1941), 28.

52. John B. Whitton, "War by Radio," *Foreign Affairs*, 19 (April 1941) 590, 594, 596.

53. Culbert, *News for Everyman*, 114.

54. Chatham House, Ronald Tree, "An American View of the War," speech delivered April 4, 1940, RIIA 8/622.

55. Joseph P. Lash, *Roosevelt and Churchill 1939–1941* (New York: W. W. Norton, 1976), 316–17.

56. Culbert, *News for Everyman*, 166.

57. Whalen, *The Founding Father*, 323, 324.

58. Whalen, *The Founding Father*, 330.

59. Beschloss, *Kennedy and Roosevelt*, 218.

60. Beschloss, *Kennedy and Roosevelt*, 219.

61. Reynolds, *From Munich to Pearl Harbor*, 101.

62. Beschloss, *Kennedy and Roosevelt*, 222–28; Whalen, *The Founding Father*, 342.

63. Joseph P. Lash, *Eleanor: The Years Alone* (New York: W. W. Norton, 1972), 287.

64. Whalen, *The Founding Father*, 347.

65. Painter-Downes, *London War Notes*, 113; Murrow, *This Is London*, 217.

66. Edward Mead Earle, *Against This Torrent* (Princeton: Princeton University Press, 1941), 14, 60.

67. John Morton Blum, ed., *Public Philosopher: Selected Letters of Walter Lippmann* (New York: Ticknor & Fields, 1985), 402, 407.

68. Sheean, *Between the Thunder and the Sun*, 312.

69. Reynolds, *From Munich to Pearl Harbor*, 108.

70. Cull, *Selling War*, 109, 225.

71. Reynolds, *From Munich to Pearl Harbor*, 124.

72. Goodwin, *No Ordinary Time*, 194; Charles Peters, *Five Days in Philadelphia* (New York: PublicAffairs, 2005), 183.

73. Churchill, *Memoirs of the Second World War*, 385.

74. Peters, *Five Days in Philadelphia*, 181.

75. FDR Library, President's Secretary's File, box 34, letter to King George VI.

76. Cannadine, *Blood, Toil, Tears, and Sweat*, 212–13.

77. Persico, *Edward R. Murrow*, 166.

78. Sperber, *Murrow*, 166.

79. MHC, JBM to families, September (no date) 1940.

80. Persico, *Edward R. Murrow*, 178, 184; Kendrick, *Prime Time*, 183; MHC, ERM letter to Brewsters, March 31, 1941.

81. Kendrick, *Prime Time*, 215.

82. MHC, JBM to families, October 22, 1940.

83. Sperber, *Murrow*, 193; Kendrick, *Prime Time*, 216.

84. MHC, JBM letter to Dart Brewster, May 7, 1941.

85. MHC, JBM letter to Florence Clement, December 1, 1940.

86. MHC, JBM speech text.

87. MHC, JBM letter to Florence Clement, December 1, 1940.

88. MHC, JBM to families, November 10, 1940, March 1, 1941; to Florence Clement, December 1, 1940.

89. MHC, JBM to Dart Brewster, no date (probably April 1941).

90. Kendrick, *Prime Time*, 208; Sperber, *Murrow*, 195; Cloud and Olson, *The Murrow Boys*, 92.

91. Kendrick, *Prime Time*, 224.

92. Robert E. Sherwood, *Roosevelt and Hopkins* (New York: Enigma Books, 2001), 230.

93. Kendrick, *Prime Time*, 226.

94. Sperber, *Murrow*, 169, 188, 195.

95. Sheean, *Between the Thunder and the Sun*, 211; Schroth, *The American Journey of Eric Sevareid*, 172, 173.

96. Kendrick, *Prime Time*, 205; Sheean, *Between the Thunder and the Sun*, 210, 211.

97. Maureen Waller, *London 1945* (New York: St. Martin's, 2004), 362–63.

98. Murrow, *This Is London*, 221, 224.

99. Murrow, *This Is London*, 228, 230.

100. Murrow, *This Is London*, 236–37.

Chapter Four

1. Cannadine, *Blood, Toil, Tears and Sweat*, 194.

2. Sevareid, *Not So Wild a Dream*, 169.

3. Sperber, *Murrow*, 182.

4. Kendrick, *Prime Time*, 218.

5. Sheean, *Between the Thunder and the Sun*, 245.

6. Bernard Bellush, *He Walked Alone: A Biography of John Gilbert Winant* (The Hague: Mouton, 1968), 121.

7. Bellush, *He Walked Alone*, 158, 160; Persico, *Edward R. Murrow*, 180.

8. Bellush, *He Walked Alone*, 160.

9. Lash, *Roosevelt and Churchill*, 280.

10. John Gilbert Winant, *Letter from Grosvenor Square* (Boston: Houghton Mifflin, 1947), 21, 25.

11. Winant, *Letter*, 28.

12. Winant, *Letter*, 132; Colville, *The Fringes of Power*, 360.

13. Winant, *Letter*, 154; John Gilbert Winant, *Our Greatest Harvest* (London: Hodder and Stoughton, 1950), 7, 16.

14. Winant, *Letter*, 90, 111.

15. Bellush, *He Walked Alone*, 173; Churchill, *Memoirs*, 417.

16. Winant, *Letter*, 64.

17. Winant, *Letter*, 95.

18. Anthony Eden, *The Reckoning* (Boston: Houghton Mifflin, 1965), 295.

19. Harold Nicolson, *Diaries and Letters 1939–1945* (New York: Atheneum, 1967), 186; Colville, *The Fringes of Power*, 773.

20. Colville, *The Fringes of Power*, 372.

21. Bellush, *He Walked Alone*, 165; Tree, *When the Moon Was High*, 157.

22. Bellush, *He Walked Alone*, 172.

23. Bellush, *He Walked Alone*, 168; Winant, *Letter*, 56, 62.

24. Winant, *Letter*, 164, 200.

25. FDR Library, letter, ERM to John G. Winant, November 10, 1941; John G. Winant collection; Box 209; Folder, Murrow, Edward R. and Janet.

26. Winant, *Our Greatest Harvest*, v.

27. BBC, RCONT1 Talks, Murrow, Edward, file 1.

28. BBC, R34/187.

29. BBC, R61/3/3.

30. *Time*, April 28, 1941, 15.

31. Sheean, *Between the Thunder and the Sun*, 248.

32. Margaret MacMillan, *Paris 1919* (New York: Random House, 2002), 132.

33. Harold Nicolson, *Diaries and Letters 1930–1939* (New York: Atheneum, 1966), 402.

34. James Lees-Milne, *Harold Nicolson: A Biography* (Hamden, Conn.: Archon Books, 1984), 124.

35. Harold Nicolson, *Why Britain Is at War* (Harmondsworth, U.K.: Penguin, 1939), 136, 150.

36. Ziegler, *London at War*, 172–73; Nicolson, *Diaries and Letters 1939–1945*, 149.

37. Nicolson, *Diaries and Letters 1939–1945*, 116.

38. Nicolson, *Diaries and Letters 1939–1945*, 130.

39. Nicolson, *Diaries and Letters 1930–1939*, 403.

40. Nicolson, *Diaries and Letters 1939–1945*, 37, 94.

41. Lees-Milne, *Harold Nicolson*, 130.

42. Lukacs, *Five Days in London*, 168; Nicolson, *Diaries and Letters 1939–1945*, 162.

43. Nicolson, *Diaries and Letters 1939–1945*, 105; Briggs, *The War of Words*, 10.

44. Nicolson, *Diaries and Letters 1930–1939*, 394; Nicolson, *Diaries and Letters 1939–1945*, 104, 109, 139.

45. James Leutze, ed., *The London Journal of General Raymond E. Lee* (Boston: Little, Brown, 1971), xiii, 370, 14.

46. Leutze, *London Journal*, 103.

47. Leutze, *London Journal*, 62, 241.

48. Leutze, *London Journal*, 58, 78, 171.

49. Leutze, *London Journal*, 138.

50. Leutze, *London Journal*, 243, 253.

51. Leutze, *London Journal*, 180, 18, 317, 383.

52. Leutze, *London Journal*, 67, 53.

53. James Reston, *Deadline* (New York: Random House, 1991), 92.

54. Leutze, *London Journal*, 391, 28.

55. Leutze, *London Journal*, 307.

56. Leutze, *London Journal*, 306.

57. Leutze, *London Journal*, 359, 360.

58. Leutze, *London Journal*, 145.

59. Leutze, *London Journal*, 57.

60. Leutze, *London Journal*, 126.

61. Leutze, *London Journal*, 25, 115.

62. Leutze, *London Journal*, 302; Sherwood, *Roosevelt and Hopkins*, 292.

63. Leutze, *London Journal*, 433.

64. Robert Rhodes James, ed., *Chips: The Diaries of Sir Henry Channon* (London: Phoenix Press, 2003), 328; Colville, *The Fringes of Power*, 134.

65. Colville, *The Fringes of Power*, 183, 203.

66. Charles Edward Lysaght, *Brendan Bracken* (London: Allen Lane, 1979), 183; Colville, *The Fringes of Power*, 331.

67. Cull, *Selling War*, 158; Lysaght, *Brendan Bracken*, 196.

68. Meacham, *Franklin and Winston*, 75.

69. Lysaght, *Brendan Bracken*, 190.

70. Lysaght, *Brendan Bracken*, 193, 196, 217; Cull, *Selling War*, 148.

71. Lysaght, *Brendan Bracken*, 194, 198.

72. Lysaght, *Brendan Bracken*, 196; John Lukacs, *The Duel* (New York: Ticknor and Fields, 1990), 215.

73. Lysaght, *Brendan Bracken*, 197; Sherwood, *Roosevelt and Hopkins*, 359; Persico, *Edward R. Murrow*, 221.

74. MHC, ERM to Harry Hopkins, November 11, 1941; ERM to Averill Harriman, November 11, 1941; Lord Halifax to ERM, November 21, 1941.

75. MHC, JBM to Brewsters, September 8, 1941.

76. MHC, ERM to Arthur Packard, October 2, 1941; Harold Laski to ERM, October 27, 1941; FDR Library, ERM to John G. Winant, November 10, 1941; John G. Winant collection; Box 209; Folder: Murrow Edward R. and Janet.

77. BBC, R 61/5.

78. MHC, H. B. Tull to JBM, July 19, 1941.

79. FDR Library, JBM to John G. Winant, (received) October 4, 1941; John G. Winant collection; Box 209; Folder: Murrow, Edward R. and Janet.

80. Sperber, *Murrow*, 198; *Time*, August 4, 1941, 15; *Time*, November 10, 1941, 51.

81. Dallek, *Franklin Roosevelt and American Foreign Policy*, 287; Frederick Whyte, Chatham House meeting, October 30, 1941, RIIA 8/768.

82. Dallek, *Franklin Roosevelt and American Foreign Policy*, 287; Yeilding and Carlson, *Ah, That Voice*, 136–37.

83. Lash, *Roosevelt and Churchill*, 419–20; Meacham, *Franklin and Winston*, 127.

Chapter Five

1. Sperber, *Murrow*, 204.

2. FDR Library, President's Personal File; Murrow, Edward R.

3. Archibald MacLeish, "A Superstition Is Destroyed," in "In Honor of a Man and an Ideal: Three Talks on Freedom," CBS, December 2, 1941, 6–7.

4. MacLeish, "A Superstition Is Destroyed," 8–9, 10.

5. Edward R. Murrow, "A Report to America," in "In Honor of a Man and an Ideal: Three Talks on Freedom," CBS, December 2, 1941, 20, 17, 21, 30, 25, 33, 31.

6. MHC, ERM to John Marshall, September 29, 1941; MHC, ERM to Harold Laski, December 6, 1941.

7. *The Times*, September 5, 1941.

8. Philip E. Jacob, "Influences of World Events on U.S. 'Neutrality' Opinion," *Public Opinion Quarterly*, 4, no. 1 (March 1940): 51–52, 58.

9. Jacob, "Influences of World Events," 55, 59; Hadley Cantril, "Public Opinion in Flux," *Annals of the American Academy of Political and Social Science*, 220 (March 1942): 137.

10. Jacob, "Influences of World Events," 59, 56, 61.

11. Gallup Poll, October 3, 1939–April 17, 1940.

12. Jacob, "Influences of World Events," 56.

13. Hadley Cantril, "America Faces the War: A Study in Public Opinion," *Public Opinion Quarterly*, 4, no. 3 (September 1940): 401, 392.

14. Cantril, "America Faces the War," 391.

15. Gallup Poll, September 17, 1940, September 30, 1940; Cantril, "Public Opinion in Flux," 137–38.

16. Cantril, "Public Opinion in Flux," 138, 146.

17. Cantril, "Public Opinion in Flux," 141, 147, 150.

18. Pyle, "Ed Murrow."

19. Cantril, "Public Opinion in Flux," 144, 145.

20. Cantril, "Public Opinion in Flux," 138.

21. Stanley Weintraub, *Long Day's Journey into War* (New York: Plume, 1992), 328.

22. FDR Library, Eleanor Roosevelt oral history; Folder: Lash, Trude.

23. "Roosevelt Surprise on Dec. 7, '41 Depicted," *New York Times*, September 24, 1945, 3.

24. Weintraub, *Long Day's Journey*, 489, 532–33; "Roosevelt Surprise"; Bliss, *In Search of Light*, 109.

25. Weintraub, *Long Day's Journey*, 533.

26. Weintraub, *Long Day's Journey*, 533; Sperber, *Murrow*, 207; Persico, *Edward R. Murrow*, 195.

27. Ronald Steel, *Walter Lippmann and the American Century* (Boston: Atlantic-Little, Brown, 1980), 107, 134; Peters, *Five Days in Philadelphia*, 158.

28. Weintraub, *Long Day's Journey*, 339–40.

29. Churchill, *Memoirs of the Second World War*, 506.

30. Archibald MacLeish, *American Opinion and the War* (New York: Macmillan, 1942), 8, 9, 27.

31. Painter-Downes, *London War Notes*, 185, 186, 191.

32. "New Ties Are Seen in Aid to England," *New York Times*, October 18, 1941, 12.

33. MHC, JM speech manuscript (undated), 1, 7–8, 11.

34. Persico, *Edward R. Murrow*, 196.

35. MHC, ERM letter and memo to E. K. Klauber, January 10, 1942.

36. Edward R. Murrow, "Notes on the Way," *Time and Tide*, July 19, 1941, 596.

37. MHC, Harold Laski letter to ERM, January 4, 1942; ERM letter to William Paley, January 16, 1942.

38. FDR Library, Harry L. Hopkins collection; Box 203; Folder: Murrow, Edward R.

39. Bliss, *In Search of Light*, 50.

40. Bliss, *In Search of Light*, 50, 53, 60.

41. Waller, *London 1945*, 107.

42. *Instructions for American Servicemen in Britain* (Washington: War Department, 1942). Republished by Bodleian Library, University of Oxford, second edition 2004.

43. Bliss, *In Search of Light*, 59.

44. Bliss, *In Search of Light*, 56, 65, 62.

45. Bliss, *In Search of Light*, 70–76.

46. Waller, *London 1945*, 21, 33.

47. Waller, *London 1945*, 13–15.

48. Waller, *London 1945*, 40, 69.

49. Ziegler, *London at War*, 297; Bliss, *In Search of Light*, 89.

50. Bliss, *In Search of Light*, 90.

51. Waller, *London 1945*, 155, 192.

52. Bliss, *In Search of Light*, 91–94.

53. Deborah E. Lipstadt, *Beyond Belief* (New York: Free Press, 1986), 244.

54. Cannadine, *Blood, Toil, Tears, and Sweat*, 256.

Selected Bibliography

Books

Bellush, Bernard. *He Walked Alone: A Biography of John Gilbert Winant.* The Hague: Mouton, 1968.

Berg, A. Scott. *Lindbergh.* New York: Berkley Books, 1999.

Beschloss, Michael R. *Kennedy and Roosevelt.* New York: Norton, 1980.

Bliss, Edward, Jr., ed. *In Search of Light: The Broadcasts of Edward R. Murrow.* New York: Knopf, 1967.

Bosco, Andrea and Cornelia Navari. *Chatham House and British Foreign Policy 1919–1945.* London: Lothian Foundation Press, 1994.

Boyle, Andrew. *Poor, Dear Brendan: The Quest for Brendan Bracken.* London: Hutchinson, 1974.

Briggs, Asa. *The War of Words.* London: Oxford University Press, 1970.

Butler, J. R. M. *Lord Lothian.* London: Macmillan, 1960.

Cannadine, David, ed. *Blood, Toil, Tears and Sweat: The Speeches of Winston Churchill.* Boston: Houghton Mifflin, 1989.

Carter, Ernestine, ed. *Bloody but Unbowed.* New York: Scribner's, 1941.

Casey, Steven. *Cautious Crusade.* New York: Oxford University Press, 2001.

Churchill, Winston S. *Memoirs of the Second World War.* Boston: Houghton Mifflin, 1959.

Cloud, Stanley and Lynne Olson. *The Murrow Boys.* Boston: Houghton Mifflin, 1996.

Colville, John. *The Fringes of Power: 10 Downing Street Diaries 1939–1955.* New York: Norton, 1985.

Culbert, David Holbrook. *News for Everyman.* Westport, Conn.: Greenwood, 1976.

Cull, Nicholas John. *Selling War.* New York: Oxford University Press, 1995.

Dallek, Robert. *Franklin D. Roosevelt and American Foreign Policy, 1932–1945.* New York: Oxford University Press, 1979.

De Courcy, Anne. *1939: The Last Season.* London: Phoenix, 2003.

Douglas, Susan J. *Listening In: Radio and the American Imagination.* New York: Times Books, 1999.

Earle, Edward Mead. *Against This Torrent.* Princeton: Princeton University Press, 1941.

Eden, Anthony. *The Reckoning.* Boston: Houghton Mifflin, 1965.

Edwards, Bob. *Edward R. Murrow and the Birth of Broadcast Journalism.* Hoboken, N.J.: John Wiley, 2004.

Gilbert, Martin. *Churchill.* New York: Henry Holt, 1991.

Goodwin, Doris Kearns. *No Ordinary Time.* New York: Simon and Schuster, 1994.

Instructions for American Servicemen in Britain 1942. Washington: War Department, 1942; reprinted, Oxford: Bodleian Library, 2004.

Jackson, Robert H. *That Man: An Insider's Portrait of Franklin D. Roosevelt.* New York: Oxford University Press, 2003.

Kendrick, Alexander. *Prime Time: The Life of Edward R. Murrow.* Boston: Little Brown, 1969.

Kennedy, David M. *Freedom from Fear.* New York: Oxford University Press, 1999.

Kimball, Warren F. *Forged in War.* New York: William Morrow, 1997.

Lash, Joseph P. *Roosevelt and Churchill 1939-1941.* New York: W. W. Norton, 1976.

Lees-Milne, James. *Harold Nicholson: A Biography* vol. 2. Hamden, Conn.: Archon, 1984.

Leutze, James, ed. *The London Journal of General Raymond E. Lee 1940–1941.* Boston: Little, Brown, 1971.

Lukacs, John. *The Duel.* New York: Ticknor and Fields, 1990.

———. *Five Days in London, May 1940.* New Haven, Conn.: Yale University Press, 1999.

Lysaght, Charles Edward. *Brendan Bracken.* London: Allen Lane, 1979.

MacLeish, Archibald. *American Opinion and the War.* New York: Macmillan, 1942.

Meacham, Jon. *Franklin and Winston.* New York: Random House, 2003.

Merz, Charles, ed. *Days of Decision: Wartime Editorials from* The New York Times. Garden City, N.Y.: Doubleday, Doran, 1941.

Ministry of Home Security, *Front Line 1940–41: The Official Story of the Civil Defense of Britain.* London: His Majesty's Stationery Office, 1942.

Murrow, Edward R. *This Is London.* New York: Simon and Schuster, 1941.

Nicolson, Harold. *Diaries and Letters 1930–1939.* New York: Atheneum, 1966.

———. *Diaries and Letters 1939–1945.* New York: Atheneum, 1967.

———. *Why Britain Is at War.* Harmondsworth, U.K.: Penguin, 1939.

Painter-Downes, Mollie. *London War Notes 1939–1945.* New York: Farrar, Straus and Giroux, 1971.

Persico, Joseph E. *Edward R. Murrow: An American Original.* New York: McGraw-Hill, 1988.

Peters, Charles. *Five Days in Philadelphia.* New York: PublicAffairs, 2005.

Priestley, J. B. *Britain Speaks.* New York: Harper and Bros., 1940.

Pyle, Ernie. *Ernie Pyle in England.* New York: Robert M. McBride and Co., 1941.

Ray, John. *The Night Blitz.* London: Arms and Armour, 1996.

Renier, Olive and Vladimir Rubinstein. *Assigned To Listen.* London: BBC External Services, 1986.

Reynolds, David. *From Munich to Pearl Harbor.* Chicago: Ivan R. Dee, 2001.

Reynolds, Quentin. *Britain Can Take It.* New York: Dutton, 1941.

———. *A London Diary.* New York: Random House, 1941.

———. *The Wounded Don't Cry.* New York: Dutton, 1941.

Rhodes James, Robert, ed. *Chips: The Diaries of Sir Henry Channon.* London: Phoenix Press, 2003.

Rock, William R. *Chamberlain and Roosevelt: British Foreign Policy and the United States, 1937–1940.* Columbus, Ohio: Ohio State University Press, 1988.

Rolo, Charles J. *Radio Goes to War.* New York: G. P. Putnam's Sons, 1942.

Rose, Norman. *The Cliveden Set.* London: Jonathan Cape, 2000.

Schroth, Raymond A. *The American Journey of Eric Sevareid.* South Royalton, Vt.: Steerforth Press, 1995.

Sevareid, Eric. *Not So Wild a Dream.* New York: Atheneum, 1976.

Sheean, Vincent. *Between the Thunder and the Sun.* New York: Random House, 1943.

Sherwood, Robert E. *Roosevelt and Hopkins.* New York: Enigma Books, 2001.

Shirer, William L. *The Rise and Fall of the Third Reich.* New York: Simon and Schuster, 1960.

Smith, R. Franklin. *Edward R. Murrow: The War Years.* Kalamazoo, Mich.: New Issues Press, 1978.

Sperber, A. M. *Murrow: His Life and Times.* New York: Freundlich Books, 1986.

Sykes, Christopher. *Nancy: The Life of Lady Astor.* London: Collins, 1972.

Taylor, Philip M. *British Propaganda in the 20th Century.* Edinburgh: Edinburgh University Press, 1999.

Tree, Ronald. *When the Moon Was High.* London: Macmillan, 1975.

Waller, Maureen. *London 1945.* New York: St. Martin's, 2004.

Weintraub, Stanley. *Long Day's Journey into War.* New York: Plume, 1992.

Welles, Sumner. *The Time for Decision.* New York: Harper and Brothers, 1944.

Whalen, Richard J. *The Founding Father: The Story of Joseph P. Kennedy.* New York: New American Library, 1964.

White, Paul W. *News on the Air.* New York: Harcourt, Brace, 1947.

Winant, John Gilbert. *Letter from Grosvenor Square*. Boston: Houghton Mifflin, 1947.

———. *Our Greatest Harvest*. London: Hodder and Stoughton, 1950.

Yeilding, Kenneth D. and Paul H. Carlson, eds. *Ah, That Voice: The Fireside Chats of Franklin Delano Roosevelt*. Odessa, Texas: John Ben Shepperd, Jr. Library of the Presidents, 1974.

Ziegler, Philip. *London at War 1939–1945*. London: Pimlico, 2002.

Articles, documents, etc.

Cantril, Hadley. "America Faces the War: A Study in Public Opinion." *Public Opinion Quarterly*, 4, no. 3 (September 1940): 387-407.

———. "Public Opinion in Flux." *Annals of the American Academy of Political and Social Science*, 220 (March 1942): 136-152.

"Editorials Back President's Plea," *New York Times*, September 22, 1939, 19.

Graves, Harold N., Jr. "European Radio and the War." *Annals of the American Academy of Political and Social Science*, 213 (January 1941): 75-82.

———. "Propaganda by Short Wave: Berlin Calling America." *Public Opinion Quarterly*, 4, no. 4 (December 1940): 601-619.

———. "Propaganda by Short Wave: London Calling America." *Public Opinion Quarterly*, 5, no. 1 (March 1941): 38-51.

"In Honor of a Man and an Ideal: Three Talks on Freedom." CBS, December 2, 1941.

Jacob, Philip E. "Influences of World Events on U.S. 'Neutrality' Opinion." *Public Opinion Quarterly*, 4, no. 1 (March 1940): 48-65.

Larson, Cedric. "The British Ministry of Information." *Public Opinion Quarterly*, 5, no. 3 (Autumn 1941): 412-431.

MacLeish, Archibald. "A Superstition Is Destroyed," in "In Honor of a Man and an Ideal: Three Talks on Freedom," CBS, December 2, 1941.

Murrow, Edward R. "A Report to America," in "In Honor of a

Man and an Ideal: Three Talks on Freedom," CBS, December 2, 1941.

Parmar, Inderjeet. "Chatham House, the Foreign Policy Process, and the Making of the Anglo-American Alliance," in Andrea Bosco and Cornelia Navari (eds.), *Chatham House and British Foreign Policy 1919-1945.* London: Lothian Foundation Press, 1994.

White, Paul W. "Covering a War for Radio." *Annals of the American Academy of Political and Social Science*, 213 (January 1941): 83-92.

Whitton, John B. "War by Radio." *Foreign Affairs*, 19 (April 1941): 584-596.

Index

Adams, Mary, 44
Against This Torrent, 100
Agar, Herbert, 159
America First Committee, 23, 24, 125, 146
American Committee for the Evacuation of Children, 53
American Home, The, 25
American Red Cross, 54
Anderson, Ida Lou, 86
Associated Press, 13, 85
Astor, John Jacob, 58
Astor, Nancy, 58–63, 64, 69, 131
Astor, Waldorf, 58
Athenia, 22

Balderston, John L., 68
Barman, Thomas, 44
Bartlett, Vernon, 72
Baruch, Bernard, 31
Bate, Fred, 85, 88
BBC Handbook, 130
Beaverbrook, Lord, 141–42
Belgium, 27, 28
Benny, Jack, 18
Berg, A. Scott, 24
Berlin, Irving, 69

Berlin, Isaiah, 69
Bevin, Ernest, 55
Bloody but Unbowed, 94
Boettiger, John, 99
Borah, William, 152
Boston Globe, 99
Bowes-Lyon, David, 126
Bracken, Brendan, 66–68, 139–43
Brazil, 67
Breckinridge, Mary Marvin, 9
Brewster, Charles, 49
Brewster, Jennie, 49
Britain Can Take It, 95
British Broadcasting Corporation (BBC), 3, 8, 18, 21–22, 34, 39, 70, 73, 84–85, 87, 94, 95–96, 163–64, 167; and American liaison, 20, 144–45; and North American Service, 35, 72; and ties to Murrow, 3, 22, 34–35, 71–72, 88, 94, 116, 124–25
British Information Service, 67–68
Buchenwald, 170–71
Bundles for Britain, 53–54, 57, 107, 137, 161

Cadogan, Alexander, 43
Campbell, Kay, 106
Canada, 35, 41, 72, 133
Cantril, Hadley, 154, 155
casualties, 77, 82, 92, 95, 168, 169
CBS, 5, 8, 10–11, 13, 35, 51, 70, 73, 87, 144, 162–64, 165; and editorial guidelines, 10, 32
censorship, 39–40, 88–89, 148–49, 163–64
Central America, 68
Century Group, 159
Chamberlain, Neville, 1, 14, 18, 19, 22, 27, 31, 59, 61, 62, 64, 115, 127, 129, 152, 158
Channels of Publicity Enquiry, 22
Channon, Henry "Chips," 61, 139
Chaplin, Charlie, 62
children: evacuation from London of, 2, 5, 17, 23, 53, 111
Church, Wells, 72
Churchill, Clementine, 57
Churchill, Winston, 1, 18, 21, 22, 28, 29, 36, 46, 57, 63–64, 67–69, 74–75, 96, 97, 118–22, 128–29, 152; and relationship with Roosevelt, 41, 159, 161, 166, 172; and speeches, 12, 18–19, 27–28, 42–43, 83, 104, 115, 129, 161, 172
Claridge's, 109, 133
Clark, Champ, 66
Cliveden Set, 58–63
"CNN effect," x
Cockburn, Claud, 59–60
Cohen, Ben, 117
Colefax, Sibyl, 101, 116
Collier's, 70–71
Collingwood, Charles, xi, 44, 111

Colville, John, 66, 118, 121, 140
Committee to Defend America by Aiding the Allies, 23
concentration camps, 25, 168, 170–71
Cooke, Alistair, 72
Cooper, Alfred Duff, 35, 66, 89, 129
Coughlin, Charles, 12, 45
Cranborne, Lord, 56
Crowther, Geoffrey, 109
Czechoslovakia, 30

Daily Express, 43–44
Daily Herald, 44
Daily Mail, 99–100
Daily Telegraph, 18
Darvall, Dorothy, 56, 108
Darvall, Frank, 21, 88, 108, 109
Davis, Elmer, 8, 26, 83, 123
Dawson, Geoffrey, 59, 60
Denmark, 27
Ditchley, 63–64, 65, 66, 106
Donovan, William, 74–75, 158
Dorchester, The, 116
Dunkirk, 28–29, 33, 149, 152, 162

Earle, Edward Mead, 100
Eckersley, Roger, 20–21, 35–36, 70, 88, 125
Economic Warfare, Ministry of, 126, 164
Eden, Anthony, 59, 60, 64, 121, 137
Edwards, Bob, 87
Elizabeth, Princess, 96
Elizabeth, Queen, 126

Farley, James A., 12
Field, Marshall, 63
Fields, Gracie, 11

Fiske, Billy, 123
Foreign Office, 31, 43, 64, 65, 73, 96, 164
Fortune, 145, 151
France, 27, 28, 37, 38, 72, 87, 163
Frankfurter, Felix, 62, 67, 109

Gable, Clark, 55
Gallup Poll, 103, 146, 153–55
Garvin, J. L., 59, 60
George VI, King, 14, 16, 74, 79, 81, 104, 118
Goebbels, Joseph, 39, 60, 130
Goldbergs, The, 35
Graebner, Walter, 141
Greer, 145–46
Grigg, Edward, 56
Grim Glory, 94

Halifax, Lord, 28, 59, 116, 118, 144
Harriman, Averill, 122, 144, 159
Haw-Haw, Lord (William Joyce), 36–37
Hearst, William Randolph, x
Hearst News, 85
Henry, Bill, 39
Herald Tribune (New York), 159
Hitler, Adolf, x, 1, 5, 12, 27, 29, 31, 35, 41, 45, 46, 58, 63, 82–83, 115, 127, 134, 136, 144, 158, 169
Home Security, Ministry of, 40, 169
Hoover, Herbert, 124
Hopkins, Harry, 94, 96, 109–10, 131, 138, 140, 143, 144, 157, 165
Hull, Cordell, 29, 30, 157

Iceland, 120

Information, Ministry of, 21, 57, 64–69, 70, 81, 87–89, 93, 95, 124, 129–30, 136, 139–43, 145
"Instructions for American Servicemen in Britain," 167
International Labor Organization, 117
International News Service, 13
International Propaganda and Broadcasting Enquiry, 21–22
Islington, Lady, 56

Jackson, Robert, 75
Japan, 155, 158, 159, 160
Jones, Jesse, 157
Jones, Tom, 61
Joyce, William. *See*, Haw-Haw, Lord

Kaltenbach, Fred, 37–38
Kaltenborn, H. V., 8, 11
Kansas City Star, 15
Keir, David, 56
Kendrick, Alexander, 111
Kennedy, John F., 98
Kennedy, Joseph P., xi, 29–33, 41, 61, 74, 97–100, 117, 128, 132, 133, 159
Kennedy, Joseph P., Jr., 98
Klauber, Ed, 162
Knox, Frank, 102, 157
kristallnacht, 151

Lash, Joseph, 156
Lash, Trude, 156
Laski, Harold, 50, 55, 117, 144, 150, 155, 164
Lee, Raymond, 75, 131–39
Lees-Milne, James, 129
Lend-Lease, 75, 102–4, 110, 118–19

LeSueur, Larry, xi, 84, 88
Lewis, Fulton, Jr., 97
Liberty, 62
Life, 134, 141
Lindbergh, Charles, xi, 23–24, 60–61, 62, 125–26, 152
Lippmann, Walter, 101, 128, 159
listening center project, 72–73
Listowel, Countess of, 55
London Sunday Express, 8
Long, Breckinridge, 99
Long, Huey, 12
Lothian, Lord, 26, 42, 60, 61, 65, 68, 132
Louisville Courier Journal, 159
Low, David, 60
Luce, Henry R., 18, 159
Luxembourg, 27

MacAdam, Carolyn, 56–57
MacAdam, Ivison, 22, 56–57
MacLeish, Archibald, 147–48, 154, 160
Masaryk, Jan, 55, 105
McCarthy, Joseph, 172
McCormick, Pat, 95
McKinley, William, x
McLuhan, Marshall, 45
Meyer, Eugene, 135, 141
Millis, Walter, 159
Milne, A. A., 150–51
Milner, Violet, 55–56, 106
Morrison, Herbert, 169
Murrow, Ethel, 49
Murrow, Janet Brewster, xi, 49–58, 104–8, 126, 144–45, 147, 156, 158, 160–62
Murrow, Lacey, 110
Murrow, Roscoe, 49
Mutual Broadcasting System, 10–11, 13, 96, 97

National Association of Broadcasters, 24
National Unemployed Workers Union, 16–17
NBC, 5, 8, 10–11, 13, 24, 85
Netherlands, The, 27, 169
Neutrality Act, 15, 152–53
Nevins, Allan, 72
New Republic, The, 25
New York Times, The, 19, 85, 134–35, 143
New Yorker, The, 92
Nicolson, Harold, 32, 60, 63, 101, 121, 126–31, 136, 142
Nobel Prize, 23
Norway, 27
Nye, Gerald, 23

objectivity, ix–x, 10, 45, 71, 73–74, 110–12, 172–73
Operation Sea Lion, 78, 82–83

Paine, Thomas, 23
Painter-Downes, Mollie, xi, 54, 92, 100, 160–61
Paley, William, 165
Panama, 68
Parsons, Godfrey, 159
Patton, George, 171
Pétain, Henri Philippe, 72
Pitt, William, 29
Poland, 1, 5, 9, 14, 19, 22, 127, 152, 162
Priestley, J. B., 34, 92–94
propaganda, 20, 34–39, 65–66, 68, 72, 81, 95, 110, 130, 165, 171, 172
public diplomacy, 68
public opinion (U.K.), 31–33, 54, 142–43
public opinion (U.S.), 22, 23, 26–

27, 28, 29, 32, 42, 46, 58, 64, 69, 96, 100, 101–3, 119, 131, 136, 145–46, 151–55, 158, 159

Pulitzer, Joseph, x

Pyle, Ernie, xi, 55, 89, 91–92

radio, 3–5, 7–15, 44–46; and audience, 3–4, 7, 8, 45, 154; and German use of, 35, 36–39; and influence, 3–4, 7, 9, 11, 14, 21, 29, 34, 39, 45–46

Raeder, Erich, 35

RCA, 13

Reading, Lady, 56

Reith, John, 66

Reston, James, 135

Reuters, 156

Reynolds News, 60

Reynolds, Quentin, 70–71, 95

Rhondda, Lady, 55, 60

Ribbentrop, Joachim von, 60

Rockefeller Foundation, 73

Roosevelt, Eleanor, xii, 42, 55, 99, 156

Roosevelt, Franklin D., 14–15, 102–104, 112, 116, 118, 131, 145–46, 147, 157–59, 172; and 1940 campaign, xii, 23, 40–42, 75, 97–99, 101–2, 116, 146, 154–55; and response to Pearl Harbor, xii, 156–58; and use of radio, 9, 12, 145, 146, 159

Royal Air Force (RAF), 47, 77–78, 83, 94, 115, 123, 153, 162

Royal Institute of International Affairs, 3, 45–46, 73

Sackville-West, Vita, 130

Saerchinger, Cesar, 49–50

Saint Paul's Cathedral, 82

Saturday Evening Post, 101

Scotland Yard, 40

Scripps-Howard, 91

Sevareid, Eric, xi, 4, 55, 71, 78, 81–82, 84, 86, 111, 158

Share Our Wealth clubs, 12

Shaw, George Bernard, 61–62, 78, 132

Sheean, Vincent, 25, 26–27, 69–70, 78, 83–84, 101, 110, 111, 126

Sherwood, Robert E., 165

Shirer, William L., 8, 35, 51, 110

Sinclair Refining Company, 70

Smith, Howard K., 4

Smith, Kate, 150

Social Security Board, 117

South America, 67–68

Soviet Union, 83, 143, 167

Spectator, The, 31, 32, 126, 127

Sperber, Ann, 147

State Department, 31, 98

Stephenson, William, 74

Stimson, Henry L., 102, 157

Strabolgi, Lord, 55

Street, Mary, 53

Sunday Express, 96

Swing, Raymond Gram, 8, 26, 96, 123

Talbot, Godfrey, 71

This Is England, 94

Thomas, Norman, 15

Thompson, Dorothy, 135

Thurber, James, 116

Time, 15, 18, 25, 46, 78, 134, 159

Time and Tide, 60

Times, The (London), 117, 134, 150–51

Transradio Press, 13

Tree, Ronald, 37–38, 57, 63–66, 74–75, 96, 106, 121–22, 127
Trout, Bob, 158
Truman, Harry, 124
Tull, H. B., 145

Udet, Ernest, 35
United Nations, 124
United Press, 13, 85

V-1 bombs, 168–69
V-2 missiles, 169–70
Vandenberg, Arthur, 152
Vansittart, Robert, 31
Variety, 8
Victoria, Queen, 59

Wallace, Henry, 123
Walpole, Hugh, 17
War Department, 137, 139
War Information, Office of, 165
"War of the Worlds, The," 3
War Office, 21, 137, 138
Ward, Barrington, 59
Warner Brothers, 95

Washington Post, The, 135, 141
Washington State University, 86, 162
Week, The, 59, 62
Welles, Orson, 3
Welles, Sumner, 41, 54
Wellington, Lindsay, 109
Wells, H. G., 116
Whalen, Richard, 30
White, Paul, 10–11, 13, 34, 40
White, William Allen, 23
Whitehead, T. North, 118
Why England Is at War, 127
Whyte, Frederick, 22, 66, 72
Williams, Douglas, 66
Willkie, Wendell, 75, 98, 99, 154
Wilson, Woodrow, 15, 159
Winant, John G., 117–24, 136, 138–39, 144, 145, 159, 167
Winchell, Walter, 24
Wood, Robert E., 146
Woollcott, Alexander, 55

Ziegler, Philip, 90, 127
Zog, King, 116

About the Author

PHILIP SEIB is the Lucius W. Nieman Professor of Journalism at Marquette University and a leading authority on the relationship between the news media and foreign policy. He is the author of *Beyond the Front Lines: How the News Media Cover a World Shaped by War*; *Campaigns and Conscience: The Ethics of Political Journalism*; *The Global Journalist: News and Conscience in a World of Conflict*; *Going Live: Getting the News Right in a Real-time Online World*; *Headline Diplomacy: How News Coverage Affects Foreign Policy*; *Taken for Granted: The Future of U.S.–British Relations*; and other books. Seib is a veteran print and broadcast journalist whose reporting about politics has won numerous awards. He lives in Brookfield, Wisconsin.